NICU

Mom:
You Make Me Brave

NICU

Mom:
You Make Me Brave

Natalie Skye

XULON PRESS

Xulon Press
2301 Lucien Way #415
Maitland, FL 32751
407.339.4217
www.xulonpress.com

Unless otherwise indicated, Scripture quotations taken from The Message (MSG). Copyright © 1993, 1994, 1995, 1996, 2000, 2001, 2002. Used by permission of NavPress Publishing Group. Used by permission. All rights reserved.

Scripture quotations taken from the Holy Bible, New International Version (NIV). Copyright © 1973, 1978, 1984, 2011 by Biblica, Inc.™. Used by permission. All rights reserved.

Paperback ISBN-13: 978-1-66287-041-5

Hard Cover ISBN-13: 978-1-66287-230-3

Ebook ISBN-13: 978-1-66287-042-2

DEDICATION

For Noah, who is my angel and inspiration in life; to Kate, who gave me the idea to write this book and encouragement through my time in the NICU; and for all my NICU moms. You are not alone. Never lose your voice. You guys are warriors.

August 26, 2019

As the sun set on the beach, I heard the waves hitting the rocks, and I thought, *This is my fairy tale. This is everything I wanted.* I was eight months pregnant, with the love of my life at our maternity shoot, excited to meet baby Noah. As the waves hit in the background, we were looking into each other's eyes while the photos were being taken. I realized for the first time I felt so alive and was so grateful to God for giving me all I ever dreamt about as a little girl. That night on the drive home, I was given clarity that this was meant for me. I wanted to tell my fiancé so badly everything I was feeling. However, I figured it was a wave of pregnancy emotions and just wanted to enjoy the night as happy as I was without crying.

September 26, 2019

I was so anxious I couldn't sit still. I knew tomorrow was the big day, and so many things were running through my mind. I wanted to be prepared for Noah, have the apartment clean, and of course prepare myself for Noah's arrival finally. All the dreams, hopes, and desires would arrive tomorrow, and I was so scared. That night I couldn't sleep. All I could think about was, *Will I be a great mom? Will Noah love me as much as I love him? Am I ready for this task of raising a baby?* I prayed so much for the Lord to give me strength, to take all my fears away. Tomorrow I would be Noah's mom, and nothing would matter anymore besides my little boy.

September 27, 2019

As we drove on the freeway, stuck in traffic for an hour, I thought this was it. I would finally have my little family and get to meet Noah. I was so overwhelmed; finally everything was happy and exciting. This was all we had talked about for nine months, and finally he was coming. Once we arrived at the hospital, I began to feel so nervous, not about Noah but about the C-section I was about to undergo due to Noah being breech. I thought of how it would feel afterward, and whether or not I would be strong enough to get up to go see Noah. I was also in fear because I knew Noah would not go to the room with me immediately; he would be placed in the NICU due to the fluid in his brain they had discovered at our five-month ultrasound. There was a big possibility that Noah would need immediate surgery on his head to remove the fluid. I prayed feverishly that Noah would be okay, that my fiancé would be there with him when I couldn't since I would be in recovery. I hoped I would heal fast enough to get to my son before he had to go through pain in this world. At 10 a.m., the nurse wheeled me into the OR. I was so nervous for the epidural shot; I kept envisioning the needle in my lower back and began to shake. Once the RN arrived, she saw how visibly nervous I looked and began to talk to me about my hobbies and news events that were currently taking place. To this day, I don't remember her name or how she looked, but I thank God she was there in that room with me. She distracted me from my fear and the chaos that was happening behind me— from doctors arguing, to setting up all the equipment, and huge needles being placed all around for me for the epidural. She held my hands and said to think of Noah while the shot was being placed in my back. I began to drift off and envision how he would look and began feeling numerous kicks in my stomach, as if he knew he was coming as well. As soon as the epidural kicked in, I began to panic. I could no longer feel the lower half of my body, and I couldn't feel Noah anymore. I felt numb and empty; I could no longer feel him inside my stomach. The nurse said it was normal and reassured me he would be out shortly and I would get to see and touch him. I was spread out on the surgery table, and they began to start cutting. The pressure on my torso felt so weird; it wasn't pain, but the most uncomfortable feeling in my stomach. While this was happening, I began to feel cramps all over my legs and told the nurse, and she stated that was normal and that I was fine. I called for my fiancé, and they immediately ran to go get him. When he came in, I felt him grab my hand. I felt a sense of relief and I knew I was safe. Just then I began to see black spots and felt sweaty and cold. I told my fiancé I felt as if I was going to faint. He informed the nurses, and they began to retrieve blood bags just in case I started hemorrhaging, and continued watching my vitals. In the distance, I heard the doctor say, "He is out," and I looked at my fiancé with fear and said,

"Why isn't he crying?" Noah wasn't crying. I couldn't hear him, and with every fiber in my body, I was trying to get up to go to him, but I couldn't move. I saw a nurse run and push a button on the wall labeled "Code white," and an alarm went off, saying "CODE WHITE IN OR 9."

Immediately nurses and doctors came rushing in. I looked at my fiancé and saw the terror on his face. I asked him to tell me what was happening, and he looked at me and said, "Nothing. Noah is okay." I held his hand tighter and told him to please stop lying to me, as I could see the pupils in his eyes enlarge as if he was terrified. He told me Noah was not breathing, but he was okay. I began praying, even though I knew we weren't supposed to bargain with God. I didn't know what else to do, so I began to pray: *Lord, take me and not him. Let him be okay. Please give him my breath.* Then we heard a cry. I opened my eyes, and both my fiancé and I were teary-eyed and smiling. Noah was okay, Noah was here, and Noah was alive; he arrived at 10:43 a.m. I began drifting off. I felt as if I couldn't keep my eyes open anymore. My fiancé then told me, "Nat, you feel so cold. Are you okay?" At this point, I couldn't talk; I felt as if I was a million miles away. I kept thinking, *Don't faint; you need to see Noah,* and my self-conscious kept informing me to think happy thoughts. I immediately went back to August 26, hearing the waves and looking into my fiancé's eyes, thinking my dream had come true. Just then a doctor told me, "We are rushing Noah to the NICU." He showed him to me for five seconds, saying, "Here's your little boy," and I smiled and cried. The doctor started to wheel Noah away. Inside, I wanted to scream for them not to take him, to please let me touch him at least; however, my blood sugar was dropping so fast all I let out were mumbles. My fiancé looked at me and said, "I don't want to leave you," but I told him, "Please go be with Noah." He looked so distraught and told me he loved me and left. I sat there feeling the pressure as they began to sew my stomach back together. I kept drifting in and out. My hearing senses kicked in, and all I could hear was the doctor's classical music playing in the background while I thought of Noah's face. I kept praying for God to keep me conscious, since I felt as if I was going to faint at any given moment. I looked around the room and spotted a poster of a family, and I continued to think to myself to focus on one thing, since the room was spinning. I immediately focused on a poster of a family and stared at the mom's face and smile, and started to drift off to the maternity shoot, being held by my fiancé all while watching the waves and us laughing like the first night we met. Suddenly my train of thought was broken by the doctor saying, "Okay, we are all done."

They began to lift me to a different bed and roll me off to the recovery room. As I was lying in the bed, still in shock at what had just occurred, I instantly became so hungry and began to beg the nurse for something to eat. She responded by letting me know I could only have ice. At that moment, I didn't care—anything sounded so good to me. As the nurse returned with a cup of ice, I shoved it into my mouth, envisioning the juiciest steak I could imagine, and for some odd reason, it satisfied my hunger. I looked at the clock and it was11:30 a.m. I immediately began to panic and started asking the nurse, "What happened to my baby? What is going on? Why wasn't he breathing?" She tried to reassure me by stating, "It happens a lot to babies"; however, I believe she was trying her best not to contribute to my worried face. Just then my aunt walked in and I asked, "How's Noah?" She responded by telling me, "He is fine. He is such a beautiful baby boy."

As the time became later, I could feel movement and sharp pain in my abdomen, and I started requesting pain medicine. Shortly after, my fiancé walked in and informed me Noah was okay. I begged him to please not leave his side. He reassured me he wouldn't and got asked to go back to the NICU to be with Noah, since one parent had to be by his bedside when there were visitors present. My nurse entered the room and told me she needed to change me. I felt so helpless; I still couldn't move my lower half, and I smelled poop in the diaper they had previously placed on me after the C-section. I was so embarrassed when she had to clean me, but from there I was wheeled away to the postpartum unit. When I arrived there, I pleaded with the nurse to allow me to go see my son, and they responded I couldn't go until I walked tonight. I cried and cried and begged for them to please wheel me over the NICU, and they responded it was protocol to rest. They informed me that I could begin to try to walk tonight, and if I could, then I could be wheeled to the NICU. As I lay there in tears alone for five minutes, my family began to come in and visit with me, and I completely broke down. I told my family I wanted my son, I wanted answers. Why wasn't he breathing? Was he okay? What were the results of the MRI? When could he come bedside with me? When my fiancé came to check on me, I asked him multiple questions, and he responded that Noah was okay; he was on oxygen right now, and his MRI would be tonight. Everyone kept saying to rest so I could heal, but I thought, *How can you rest when your son is nowhere near you, when there are no answers, when you are meant to be protective and be there for your child and you can't?* I lay there in utter shock and sadness, counting the minutes and continually asking the nurses, "When can I get up to walk?"

Around 9 p.m., the nurse gave me pain medicine and said, "Okay, let's try to walk." When I tried to stand up, it felt as if my torso was tearing. I cried so much but fought through it. Nothing was going to keep me from my son—nothing. I fought through the tears and stood up and began to take one step at a time. Shortly after, my fiancé came, and I was able to be wheeled over to the NICU. Once I arrived there, I felt sudden terror, hopelessness, and sadness. There lay my son with tape all over his cheeks to keep the oxygen line around his nose, intubated and panting for air as if he couldn't breathe. The NICU nurse explained that we could not hold him until he was no longer intubated. I broke into tears. My son had entered this world purple and had to be resuscitated to breathe; my son had been poked in the hand and foot with IVs five minutes after he entered this world. He did not get to feel my warmth or hear my voice until twelve hours after he was born, and yet here I was helpless, still not able to provide a safe feeling and skin-to-skin like a mother should provide instantly. I touched him through the holes in the intubated bed. I looked at him and said, "Hello, Noah," and he immediately began to wail and move his hands. I felt as if I had done something wrong to him, and my eyes became teary. The nurse commented, "He hears mom and wants to be held." I looked at her, and my heart shattered. My son was crying for me; my son had experienced pain and wanted his mom, and I could not touch him. I hung my head and broke into tears and begged my fiancé to wheel me back to my room. I felt I was just hurting my son by not being able to carry him when he wanted me. His wailing for me pierced my heart when I couldn't do anything but watch. Just then the nurses began to take him to the MRI, and I told my fiancé to go with him so he wouldn't be alone. Once the nurse wheeled me back to my room, I cried and cried for hours until my eyes were swollen. I felt guilty to know I couldn't be strong and be there for my son. I couldn't stay by his bed because I felt so worthless that I couldn't provide the comfort he needed. I was so broken that I began to pray to God to take away these feelings of guilt and to make me strong enough to be there by my Noah's bedside even though he was screaming for me. That night I stayed in my bed in fear of going back and having him cry out for me. The pain was so unbearable each time I moved that I just wanted to lie there. It made me furious that I couldn't shower or use the restroom without assistance. My mom and fiancé had to wipe me and bathe me because I couldn't bend over.

The next morning, I woke up and wheeled myself to the NICU. I didn't want to wait for anyone to push me. When I arrived there, my son was asleep. I began to sing "You Are My Sunshine," and that became our song. I prayed over and over for good results; I didn't want him in surgery and wanted him home. It was day two in the NICU. Just then the neurologist stepped in and asked to speak with me. Here it was—this was what I had been dreading. She sat me down and showed me the MRI and stated the fluid was gone and we would not be needing surgery. I immediately sighed in relief and thanked Jesus for being there for us. However, she said Noah's cerebellum was not properly formed because of the fluid that had been there and they couldn't predict how this would delay him, but they were thinking this might be the reason he couldn't breathe on his own. I sat there in shock, thinking, *He can't breathe on his own?* I didn't know this was occurring. I thought the oxygen that was placed on him was just to help for a little while until he obtained the rhythm to breathe on his own. I spoke with the NICU doctor, and he explained everything to me. He stated Noah couldn't breathe on his own for some reason, but they were doing tests to figure out why this was occurring. They had placed an oxygen line so he could receive the oxygen he was lacking. Noah had continued to clamp down and turn purple, so they had to bag him. Right then and there, I saw Noah screaming and clamping down while he stayed limp and turned a dark purple. Immediately the monitors started beeping, and nurses ran over to increase his oxygen and rub his head to stimulate him. When that didn't work, they started to use an oxygen mask to provide air until he returned to a pinkish color. I found out this had been happening since last night. The doctor told me Noah would have to do a sleep study so they could determine what was going on, and it would be a couple of days before he could do the study. I asked if I could get discharged in four days instead of three and they granted it, since Noah was in the NICU. They also told me they had tried to bottle-feed him and noticed it was lingering in his mouth and coming out from his nose, so they wanted to conduct a swallow test to make sure he was not aspirating. They had now placed a feeding tube through his nasal canal until further notice. I sat there numb, looking at my son, trying to wrap my head around what was happening. Even though I told my fiancé and family that I was fine and hopeful, I felt like a mess inside. I begged God each night to sacrifice myself in exchange for Noah. Now, I know you're not supposed to bargain with God, but I was desperate. I wanted nothing bad to happen to my son. Just then I heard a monitor go off again and saw my son crying and instantly turning purple. Nurses raced in and started bagging him, where he started to return to his normal color. I stood back in shock, not knowing what was happening and in shock of seeing my son turn completely purple. Just then I realized how severe this was; Noah was having trouble breathing and living in this world, and there was not a darn thing I could do about it.

On the third day, the doctors told me they had found protein in my urine and needed me to stay one more day to find out what was happening. I agreed; I would be closer to my son, so I was happy. That day I was finally able to hold my son, and he opened his eyes. I cried like a baby; it was as if he knew his mom was finally here with him. I apologized over and over to him, asking him to forgive me, and how sorry I was that I couldn't be there the first two days of his life. The doctors informed us it would be the next day when Noah would be transported to another Kaiser in Fontana to do a sleep study. We told them we would meet Noah at the hospital and visit him there, since I was getting discharged the next day. From then on, an urgency kicked in to look for a hotel. I didn't want to go home and enter my son's room with him not in it. I cried, pleading with my fiancé to not go home. We applied for the Ronald McDonald House and prayed God would bless us so that we would be able to stay close to Noah. I went back to my room feeling defeated. I couldn't go with my son in the transport, and I had to face the fact that this study could determine what was really going on. Upon entering my room, the nurses informed me they needed to do a routine catheter for urine tests that night to see if the protein in my urine had increased. Now mind you, I couldn't walk properly; I still needed assistance to use the restroom and shower, to get in and out of bed, had to have blood drawn every three hours to make sure nothing bad was occurring; and now I needed to have a routine catheter placed in me. Meanwhile, I was dealing with the fact that my son was in the NICU turning purple, which seemed like almost every hour. I kept reciting the verse "For when I am weak, You are strong" because I felt so much pain physically and mentally. I wanted to crawl into fetal position and give up, but when I pictured my fiancés and Noah's face, I realized I had to fight. I was robbed of holding my son on arrival, of doing skin-to-skin, of breastfeeding him, of getting to go home and enjoy him. This whole thing of a fairy tale and bringing life into this world had been an utter nightmare. I didn't know why this was happening, what I had done to deserve this, and immediately I began questioning God. *Why? It's unfair. Why are You letting Noah suffer? Why does the woman in the next room to me get to have her baby and I don't? Why are other women getting discharged with their baby, and not me? Did I do something to deserve this? Did I do something during the pregnancy that affected Noah? Did we argue too much while I was pregnant?* All these questions, and none were answered. I thought of Job, and I now understood why he was furious with God, why he questioned Him, how he felt completely abandoned and just wanted to know why. I immediately felt guilt for questioning God; I had no right to.

That night I was able to finally learn how to change his diaper and hold him. While holding him each night, I always told him he was my miracle, that I was sorry this was all happening and I couldn't protect him. I asked for a sign from God, for Him to please show me He was here in the midst of all things. I prayed that God would play with Noah and have His angels surrounding his crib when I couldn't. Right when I said that prayer, I looked up and noticed Noah's bed number was thirty-three. Now, thirty-three had always been my lucky number, my basketball jersey number, and it had always been my go-to number in everything. Right then I knew, *Okay, Lord, You are here,* and I begged for forgiveness for thinking He had abandoned me and left me alone.

October 2, 2019

Today was the day of my discharge. I woke up bright and early to go see Noah before he left for Fontana for the sleep study. He was able to eat, and I was able to touch him and hold his hand. Just then they began getting him ready for transport. When they took him, they said they would send a text letting us know he had arrived safely. My fiancé and I grabbed our things, and they told me they had to discharge me by wheelchair, that I couldn't walk out by myself per hospital policy. So there I was, being wheeled down with another mom in the elevator who was holding her baby and being discharged, while I was being discharged with a Simba, Noah's stuffed animal. You can imagine what I felt inside, which was a sense of hopelessness. I began to become so bitter and continued to feel again how unfair this was. Why were other moms going home with their babies, and not me? I had to keep my brave face on. I didn't want my fiancé knowing how I was truly feeling, how one word or one glimpse of something bad could break me down into depression. As soon as I entered the car, I broke down and sobbed. We were supposed to be going home, but now I was being discharged after five days, without Noah with us. My fiancé pleaded with me to go eat at a restaurant to have some normalcy. But to be frank, it was a way to get our minds off the fact that Noah was in an ambulance being transported to another hospital, where a study would show the truth about what was happening with him. We ate at my favorite restaurant, but my mind was not there. Every feeling of guilt was there. How could I be eating and enjoying myself when Noah was in an ambulance? I felt like a terrible mom. I felt deep in my heart that if Noah was suffering, then I should be too. My fiancé saw it all over my face and tried to cheer me up. That was another issue I felt guilty about. My fiancé had mentally lost his partner, and no matter what he did, I just saw doom and gloom. It wasn't fair to him, but I couldn't shake it. I didn't know how. I just knew I was in depression; I didn't want to be touched or loved, and wanted to be alone. All I wanted was Noah, and that's where I failed my fiancé. He wanted his loving partner to go through the storm with him, but I was depressed and gave him more to worry about. I added more to his plate; however, it was no one's fault. It wasn't fair for either of us. We were supposed to be each other's crutch, but I couldn't be that for him. I didn't know how, and I was terribly sorry for it.

As we entered Fontana Kaiser, I was still at my weakest point of not being able to fully walk correctly or able to sit comfortably. I pushed through and walked as fast as I could to the NICU. When we arrived, I saw my son in his hospital crib; there were multiple wires across his body and a monitor. The nurse informed us we could not hold him due to the test being conducted, and we must not disturb him while he was sleeping. At that point, we sat there in silence, not knowing what to do. We talked in whispers so our son wouldn't hear our voices and wake up. We both agreed to go back home and try to rest, then head back to Hollywood as soon as he arrived back at Kaiser Sunset. We were going to have to look for hotels to stay in so we could be closer to Noah until we heard back from the Ronald McDonald House. As we left the hospital, my eyes immediately teared up and I couldn't breathe. I stopped to break down. My fiancé held me and told me to let it out, and again I began to state how it killed me to leave him, and it wasn't fair. I felt like collapsing, but I did my best to zone out the negative thoughts I was thinking and focus on what my fiancé was saying: "We are going to be okay. Noah is in a safe place, and it's okay to feel this way, but we have to stay strong." I agreed it wouldn't do any good to give up, not for Noah or our family. As we continued our journey home, I told my fiancé to take me to my mom's house. I felt better sleeping there than going back to our home and seeing his vacant nursery. The last time I was in the apartment, I had envisioned walking back in with Noah, and I couldn't bring myself to enter a home where my baby was not with me. I cried the whole way home in silence, looking out the window. I thought about how naive I was to think that I would be going home three days later with my son and living happily ever after. As we entered our city, it didn't feel like home; it felt like an unfamiliar place. I entered my mom's home, went straight to bed, and prayed all night on my knees. I begged God for there to be nothing wrong with Noah and to make him strong enough to breathe on his own. I prayed for him to come home and be in our arms, where he should have been. I tried my best to sleep, but I couldn't at that point. I was sleeping four hours a day and waking up in and out of naps. Finally, I closed my eyes, and instantly I could hear the beeping of the machines, his monitor alarming us, letting us know he wasn't breathing. It was as if the sound was going to stick around and haunt me forever.

That morning I woke up and tried my best to enjoy the day. I was feeling a little better, when I immediately began to get a massive headache and see spots. I raced over to my apartment and checked my blood pressure; the machine revealed it was sky high at 169. I rushed to urgent care, where they set up an IV in my arm in case I needed fluids and blood work done. The nurse came in, began to strike up a conversation about life, and began to talk to us about Jesus. She started to talk about how sometimes we need to be grateful and not take things for granted with our blessings. She saw my face hang low, and I began to tell her our situation. I told her our son was in the NICU and we hadn't been really able to see him, and the worst part was, we didn't know why he wasn't breathing on his own. She immediately apologized and asked if she could pray over us. Right then and there, I knew it was another sign from God showing us He was there for us, He did see what was going on, and we were not alone. Just then the doctor walked in and stated, "We must admit you. We don't want you going into a seizure, and you need a magnesium drip." I explained to the doctor that I couldn't be admitted into the Antelope Valley Hospital. I informed the doctor I needed to get back to my son, who was admitted in Kaiser Sunset in Los Angeles. He stated, "We can't let you go down there unless you sign a waiver claiming you are refusing medical attention and are going against medical advice." I told them I would drive straight down to Kaiser Sunset ER and let them know what was occurring. I did this so I could be admitted into the same hospital as Noah and not be an hour and a half away. I signed the waiver, and the nurse taped my arm with the IV. She looked at me sincerely and urged me to go straight to the ER. My fiancé drove as fast as he could while trying to remain calm so I wouldn't freak out. I told him, "I'm okay. Everything is fine, and God is here with us." The whole car ride, we listened to worship music. We had an hour to kill, and from the look on my fiancé's face, he was more worried than I was. We arrived at the ER at Sunset and expressed what had occurred, and they immediately admitted me. Just then I got a phone call stating Noah had returned to the NICU in Sunset and was safe and sound asleep. She informed us we could see him whenever we were available. I thanked God and was extremely happy Noah was okay. When we arrived at the Sunset ER, they immediately rushed me to a room. The doctor walked in and told me, "You need to be placed on a magnesium drip. You'll be admitted for the next two days until the preeclampsia goes away." I nodded in agreement and thought, *At least I am across the hallway from my son.* The doctor explained to me what would occur while being on the magnesium drip. The doctor informed me I couldn't eat and would be on a liquid diet, and the worst part of all was I couldn't leave to go to the NICU until the drip was done. My eyes began to water, and inside I was screaming, *No, I was barely able to see my son, and now he is being taken away from me again!* I explained that I understood, and they wheeled me back to my old room. I sat there mortified, looking at my fiancé, pleading with him to go be with Noah so he would know one of us was there. My fiancé didn't want to leave me alone; he could see how broken and defeated I was. I put on my brave face and told him, "I am fine. I know I have to take care of me, and I know Noah is okay in the NICU." Every word I said out loud cut me to my core. I knew I was lying, but I had to say and do what I had to in order to have him there with Noah. As soon as my fiancé kissed me good-bye, I let down my wall and cried. I was alone again without my son, no mother to comfort him, no skin-to-skin, no breastfeeding. I was alone in a hospital room. I hoped and prayed my son was not crying out for me or missing me, and knew he had a mom who loved him and was there. That night I tried my best to sleep. I figured if I just slept until the magnesium drip was over, I would wake up, and everything would be done, and I could go see my son again. But boy, was I wrong.

That night they had to draw my blood every five hours to see if there were still enzymes in my blood. I also had a catheter placed in me to get an accurate urine sample to see if there was still protein in my urine. I remember looking at the time and it was 11 p.m. I heard a knock on the door for another blood draw. I physically, mentally, and emotionally was beaten up again. All I could do was hum songs of worship and think of Bible verses, such as "Never will I leave you; never will I forsake you." By the time it was 12 a.m., I couldn't even keep my eyes open. I turned on a Bible audio app and fell asleep. I woke up at 5 a.m. for another blood draw. At that time, my fiancé was back in the room, asleep on the sofa couch. I felt so hungry; however, I was on a liquid diet, so I was not looking forward to chicken broth and Jell-O for breakfast. I begged the a.m. nurse for a shower; I felt so dirty from the catheters being inserted, from blood still leaking due to the C-section. However, I had to wait for the IV to be taken out of my arm. I tried to turn on the TV to pass time, but all I could think about was Noah, how he was alone at this time in the NICU and should be here at the bedside with me. I cried and just prayed for God to remove the thoughts racing through my head of how bad of a mother I was. I prayed vigorously to keep the enemy from making me believe these thoughts. I turned on the Bible app again, and there it was, on the story of Job. For the first time, I felt that I could relate to him. I felt beaten down physically, and I felt my son and world had been taken from me and I didn't know why. At that moment, I wanted to question God and ask Him, "Why me? Why Noah?" I was supposed to be home enjoying my bundle of joy, but instead, I was hooked up to an IV to prevent seizures and still didn't know what was fully wrong with Noah. I asked God to make me brave and strong, and I constantly asked for forgiveness for questioning Him. I was just a human being questioning a god, my God. I felt so ashamed and tormented about the things I was feeling and thinking. How could I call myself a Christian when I felt my God was punishing me? I prayed for forgiveness, strength, and courage to get up and keep going even though inside my heart was breaking. At 2 p.m., I finally gathered the strength to walk around, since I was still healing from the C-section. I couldn't stay in one position, so I got off the bed and walked around the room. My fiancé then came back from visiting Noah and told me he was fine, and that the doctors were waiting for me to get off the IV so they could inform us about the results of the sleep study. I didn't want to ask any more questions because the look on his face revealed he knew something already but was waiting for me to hear it firsthand. He told me Noah opened his eyes occasionally and sometimes peeked to see who was there. I was relieved to hear some good news; for one week straight, Noah had opened his eyes for just fifteen minutes a day. Why? We didn't know. The ophthalmologist checked his eyes and revealed to us that he was not blind and could see perfectly fine. I was so happy, I praised God over and over, but now I was trying to understand whether Noah was choosing not to open his eyes or whether it was a neurological or muscular issue. It was now 5 p.m. To pass the time, I opened my Priscilla Shirer study titled *Gideon* and zoned the world out. I pretended as if nothing was going on in my life besides what I was trying to study. At that moment, I felt God was speaking to me through this study. Priscilla Shirer said something that resonates in me to this day. I'll try my best to recite it correctly, but she stated that as Christians we are often looking for a miraculous purpose in our lives, something as big as Gideon leading an army to victory or Moses parting the Red Sea. But our calling or our purpose can be as simple as raising a child. She went on to state that raising a son in this broken world to be God-driven is a hard task of its own, but it may simply be our purpose in raising our children. Right then and there, I felt peace and started to relate to what she was saying. I began praying to myself, *God, You have given me Noah because You knew I would be strong enough and faithful enough to handle this task.* At that moment, I felt the motivation to stand up and smile for the first time. I felt no matter what happened, I could do this with and through Christ Himself. My last final hours on the magnesium drip, my IV blew out, so the nurses had to place another IV in me to continue the medication. However, since my veins were now black and blue from all the blood drawn in both arms, they had to place another IV on the top of my hand. I knew the pain would increase since it was a sore area, but I was at a point wanting it to be over so I could be finished and go be with my son. After six failed attempts of trying to insert the IV in my hand (due to my being dehydrated), they were finally able to get the IV in. At 7 p.m., they turned off the drip and taped up my hand so I could shower. They didn't want to remove the IV in case I needed more medicine. At that time, I couldn't grip anything because of how weak I was in my arms due to the IV and blood draws, and my abdomen was still burning. I continued to feel a sharp pain every time I stood up or sat down. I asked my fiancé if he could help me shower and use the restroom; I felt so helpless to have someone bathe me and wipe me because I was so weak. All my life, I had so much pride in knowing I could do things on my own; it made me feel brave and strong. However, for the first time, I had no pride, no strength, and I could say I was truly vulnerable and humbled in that moment. After my shower, I was able to eat and finally head toward the NICU to see Noah. I still couldn't fully walk correctly, but slowly but surely, I made it down the hallway to the NICU. Right when I entered the ward, I heard a baby crying. I immediately thought it was Noah, and I began running down the hall. However, once I entered his pod, I realized it wasn't him; he was peacefully sleeping. I asked the nurse if I could hold my son and do skin-to-skin. I sat down and was finally able to hold my son again. I was trying so hard not to cry. I didn't want Noah feeling overwhelmed and sad by my presence. I fought back tears as I held him tight to me and kept saying I was sorry—sorry I couldn't be there for him, sorry I wasn't there for days, sorry I couldn't breastfeed him, sorry I couldn't be there to hold and care for him when he cried out. I immediately prayed and asked God to take away all the emotions so I could enjoy holding my son rather than waste it on guilt and shame. I looked around the room, looking for some sign of peace from God. I felt so alone in this. I had never been the one to ask for a sign, but as I held my son, I felt I needed to know we were safe, and that He was here with Noah when I couldn't be. (Side note: My favorite number has always been thirty-three. It had been my basketball number since the seventh grade. I would write thirty-three on my shoes all the time because it was Kobe Bryant's high school number, who was my idol.) As I held Noah and looked around the room, I noticed his bed number was thirty-three again. Right then and there, I knew it was a sign from God again showing me He was here. I wanted to cry at that moment. For the first time, I didn't feel alone. For the first time, I received the sign I had been asking for all along even though deep down inside I knew God hadn't abandoned me. That night I held Noah for as long as I could until 10 p.m. I could have stayed longer, but my body was so weak I felt I was going to fall asleep while holding him. I sang him "You Are My Sunshine" and laid him in his pod. I was finally beginning to feel okay—not good, but okay to walk out of the NICU and back to my hospital bed without my son. As we were walking out, the MD for the night stated they would go over the results with us tomorrow morning. He also informed us Noah had been sleeping, was stable, and drinking five milliliters from the bottle. I was so happy to know he was doing okay with the bottle, and that my son was getting better day by day. That night we walked hand in hand back to my hospital room, and that night I finally felt hopeful we were on the right track and Noah would be with us soon. Even though I didn't know what the results were, I figured I would enjoy this night and see it as a victory for myself.

October 6, 2019

At 5 a.m., I woke up after my blood was drawn and began to get ready for the day. I let my fiancé sleep in. I knew if he woke, he would try to persuade me to get more rest, so I snuck out of my room and informed the nurse I was headed to the NICU to see Noah. Once I arrived, I saw Noah lying there peacefully. At this time, my son was still opening his eyes for only fifteen minutes a day, sometimes more, but I was yet to see his eyes open. I tried my best to sing and calm him to let him know his momma was there. I asked to hold him, and I sat there for three hours with Noah, talking to him about how I was and how I was doing better. I told him I was praying for him, and he was going to be okay. I held my hand over his head and prayed for God to heal him, for him to get better, and, most of all, for him to come home. At 8 a.m., I placed Noah back in his bed and headed back to my room and ordered breakfast. Since I was off the liquid diet, I could now order regular food. I was so happy to finally eat breakfast. That morning I ordered coffee, French toast, eggs, and potatoes. I was happy to taste food again even if it was hospital food. After eating I called the nurse, hoping to remove the IV, since I still had a needle placed in my arm in case my results came back showing more protein in my urine. When the nurse came in at 9 a.m., she informed me I was now stable and could have the IV removed. I was ecstatic—no more blood draws, no more catheters, and full access to my son. I asked the nurse if I could be discharged around noon so I could go visit my son after a shower and find out the results I was secretly dreading. Around 11 a.m., we walked to the NICU, hoping and praying for some good news, or at least a date of when my son could come home. As soon as we arrived there, the doctors and residents were doing a debriefing in Noah's pod and asked to speak with us. The doctor informed us that the sleep study revealed that due to Noah's Dandy Walker variant, his brain was not sending signals to his lungs to breathe. Instead of breathing thirty-two times a minute, Noah's brain was signaling to his lungs to breathe only eight times a minute. I immediately began to ask every question that was on my mind: Could this be fixed? Would his brain begin to stimulate and send signals to his lungs as he got older? What was the outcome? And when could he come home? Once I saw the doctor's face, which was a wave of sadness and compassion, I knew right then and there Noah wasn't going anywhere, and the answers I was looking for, they didn't have. My eyes began to tear, and I asked the simple question, "What is the next step then?" She informed me they would be having a team meeting to discuss the future for Noah. Once the specialists discussed and formed a plan, they would like to set up a meeting with us to discuss where to go from here. The doctor then informed me to be expecting Noah to stay at least two weeks. Once she said that, I became numb. I knew I would have to live out here for the next two weeks because there was no way I was leaving that city without Noah in my arms. I then asked her if there was hope for Noah, if there was any way he would be able to breathe on his own. The doctor responded, "I can't answer that. All we can do is wait and see and hope for the best." I didn't want to cry or scream out because I was still next to Noah's crib and in front of everyone. But at that moment, my knees wanted to buckle, and I wanted to curl up in a fetal position and cry my eyes out. I turned to Noah and whispered it was okay, and that God was watching over him. I sang "You Are My Sunshine while I held his little hand. From that moment, I knew our lives would change forever.

We finally received the call to check into the Ronald McDonald House. I was able to gain some happiness from knowing how blessed we were to get a room so close to the hospital and to receive a free meal once a day. When we finally gathered our things in the room, I asked my fiancé for food. I told him how hungry I was and asked if he could please get us food. But deep down inside, I was harboring so much hurt that I felt I needed to be alone, take a shower, and bawl my eyes out. He kept asking me if I was sure I didn't want to come so I wouldn't be alone, but at that moment in time, my body and mind were so beaten up, I felt no energy to even walk to the shower. Once he left the room, I sat on the bed in complete silence, trying to process and take in everything that was happening to my life, to baby Noah. I looked back at my baby shower pictures, thinking about how happy I was to bring my little boy into this world and how I had never imagined this would be occurring. I had thought I was going to leave the hospital with Noah and have a happy, normal life. I sat there remembering how I had envisioned Noah home with me in his crib, me dressing him in his newborn outfits, him being able to do the basic milestones, and yet here I was in the unknown while my son fought to breathe every minute. I lay there and cried; I screamed out in agony, holding my chest, because for the first time ever, I felt my heart was truly shattering inside me and there was nothing I could do to fix it or save my son. That was the most painful thought: not being able to protect my son or help him find a solution. It was impossible for any human to fix, so I knew from then on all I could do was believe and have faith. I kept repeating to myself, *I believe in a God who creates miracles, and what we need is a miracle.* I didn't know what verse it was, but I instantly remembered the verse, "Come to Me, all you who are weary and burdened, and I will give you rest. Take My yoke upon you and learn from Me, for I am gentle and humble in heart, and you will find rest for your souls. For My yoke is easy and My burden is light" (Matt. 11:28–30 NIV). I remembered a pastor preaching in one of his sermons that because Jesus carries the yoke along for us, we must do everything humanly possible we can to help our situation, and then give the rest to Jesus to do what He can. For the first time ever, I realized that everything I had gone through as a child to now was all leading up to this very moment. I thanked the Lord for giving me strength and hope. I stood up and said, "I can fight this battle, for if the Lord is with me, who can stand against me?"

The next morning, I began focusing on how to increase my milk supply. I had very little, since I wasn't able to do skin-to-skin with Noah. I wrote a list of things I could do, from eating oatmeal, to pumping every three hours for fifteen minutes, to drinking a gallon of water each day, even taking Noah's blanket home with me to smell it and pretend that he was there with me. However, I was only making fifteen milliliters of breast milk, which wasn't even enough to cover one of Noah's feedings. I felt so stressed out because I knew that my son needed every drop of breast milk to help him, and yet I couldn't produce. I felt less of a woman, so during this time, I began getting down on myself for not being able to give Noah the only thing that I could at that moment, and that was breast milk. In the NICU, moms would bring bags and bags of breast milk for their babies, even sometimes having to take some home because their storage was full, and here I was only giving two bags a day for an eight-feeding day. I didn't want to envy any mom in the NICU because I knew each mom had her own heartache and story to tell. No mom wanted to be in the NICU; everyone wanted to go home with their baby, and every story was different. I had to remind myself repeatedly about these things; however, I still secretly wished I could be that mom who produced a lot of milk. As much as I hate to admit it, I often got teary-eyed and sad over someone else's joy. I felt guilty for doing this, so I would immediately close my eyes and pray for forgiveness and ask God to help me see the positive and know that I would get there. During this time, Noah was being fed five milliliters in a bottle. I was able to feed him once or twice. I was so happy, filled with joy when I was able to sit with my son and feed him. However, one time we noticed Noah began to cough up milk and choke, which led him to aspirate a little and spit up the milk. When the doctors were informed of this, they immediately stopped all feeds until they could conduct a swallow study to ensure Noah was not aspirating. That evening his doctor informed me that the next morning Noah would go have the swallow test to find out if he could continue feeding and to see if there were any other lingering issues they didn't know about. I was concerned, but I felt at ease about it. The doctors informed me I could be present during the study, but I would have to wait outside the pod. I knew I wasn't strong enough to even stand there while knowing a medical procedure was being done, and that was another issue I felt extremely guilty about. I couldn't be strong enough for Noah and be there with him during procedures; it was his dad who had to step in and hold Noah's hand while I stepped away. I couldn't be there even when they gave him his shots, when they performed a blood gas every morning by poking his foot with a needle and pressing against the palm of his foot over and over until they could fill a tube of blood, or when his IV no longer worked because his vein was shot so they had to search for a new vein and prick him over and over on his hands and feet until they found a good vein. When they placed a feeding tube through his nose so he could eat in order to avoid aspiration, and sometimes it would get pulled out on accident, leaving them to have to replace it again down his nose; or when they had to do an EEG, where tape, gauze, and wires were placed all over his head, even to the point of the tape being stuck to his hair (an EEG was done to make sure Noah was not seizing, since Dandy Walker was known to cause episodes of seizures); or when they had to swaddle him tight, since he would kick and fight if medical gloves touched him; or when the nurses checked his eyes, forcing his eyelids open in order to make sure he wasn't blind, since he refused to open them, I couldn't be there. All these things I was never there to witness when they were occurring because I was too weak-minded and felt I would cry and break down due to witnessing what my son was going through. It ate at me each day, on how could I be that mother who wasn't there, how he needed me, and yet I was in the corner crying, feeling sorrow for him instead of telling him everything was going to be okay. He was just a week old, and he had experienced so much trauma, and there was nothing I could do as a mother to protect him. Those images and guilt kept me awake most nights.

That night after visiting Noah for a few hours until 8 p.m., my body was ready to shut down. Once I lay down to rest, I immediately began getting a panic attack where I couldn't breathe, and my anxiety was sky high. My mind began racing a hundred thoughts a minute, thinking about all the worst situations Noah could be in. I felt I was drowning; a dark wave passed over me, and I broke down. I cried and cried and cried uncontrollably to the point where I felt like dying. For some reason, I couldn't shake it off, and I began thinking of ways I could end it all for me. Yes, as much as I hate to be vulnerable, I began to be overwhelmed with suicidal thoughts. I felt as though I was suffocating, and I had no way of escaping. My fiancé saw I was crying, and I began telling him how I felt and to please hold me because this dark feeling was overwhelming me. He held me and said, "You can't leave us. Noah needs you, I need you, we can't do this without each other." I cried and cried to the level of exhaustion. The next day, I slept in. After getting up, I looked in the mirror and told myself, "You can overcome this, and God is here." I opened my Bible and began reading the verse of the day and put on worship music. For some reason, that day I kept singing a song in my head, "You Make Me Brave" by Bethel Music. I don't know where I had heard it before, but the lyrics of the song kept reciting in my head. I rushed to get ready to check on Noah. Once I arrived there, they told me he had a few desaturation episodes, so they had to remove the oxygen and put him on a hospital ventilator to increase the oxygen level. They explained that the ventilator would force air into Noah's nose, which would force him to breathe, especially when he became angry and held his breath while crying. This is when I first experienced condensation, and how much I disliked it. The hospital ventilator caused a lot of condensation or water in the tubing, since the room temperature was always cold. Why was this bad? It was due to the fact that if the tubing was lifted and not cleared of the water inside, it would go down Noah's nose, immediately causing him to feel as if he were choking, and would lead to desaturation. The first time I saw this happen, I was overwhelmed with sadness, so infuriated as to why the nurses were not taking the necessary precautions to make sure that the water did not leak into Noah's nose, especially as he was being turned around to be changed and moved from side to side. Around 10 a.m., the doctors came in and wanted to discuss a meeting that would be held with all Noah's specialists to go over what the next steps would be for Noah. They told me this meeting was urgent because they had been over-seeing his chart and noticing that he was having excessive desaturations, and they were afraid he was not receiving the appropriate oxygen levels through those episodes, which would cause other health issues down the line. Once they informed me about this, I was so confused. No one knew why this was happening, and every medical professional was informing me that another medical condition might be causing this, since the Dandy Walker variant itself would not cause respiratory issues this critical. I spoke with the resident doctor that day and asked if he could give me a plan of what would be happening, so I could be ready. He began to tell me that after a meeting with his colleagues, they discussed possible solutions for Noah. They brought up oxygen to take home, depending on a decrease in desaturations. They also mentioned a possible trach. At the time, I had no idea what a trach was or why that even was an option; however, he told me we would need to set up a meeting with all the specialists and a social worker so we could all be on the same page on how to treat Noah and how to get him home ASAP.

That day I left to go back to the Ronald McDonald House early. I realized I hadn't eaten, and I wanted to be refreshed and restored, especially with the news that was recently given to me. At the Ronald McDonald House, a local church was handing out free meals to help the families who were living there. I didn't want to go. I didn't feel like being around others, but I was extremely hungry, so I decided to go. Once I was there, I realized how many families were going through a hardship as I was, and for the first time, I didn't feel alone. Everyone had a child with a medical condition—some severe, some less—but either way, they all had a story to tell and pain of their own.

As I sat at a table alone, I began to look up trach babies on the internet, and I began to get teary-eyed. For the first time in my life, I saw a trach and a hole in a baby's neck, with the baby living off a machine. I lost my appetite and went to my room and sobbed. Why was this happening? It was not fair to Noah. Why did he have to have a hole in his neck? Why did he have to be on a machine all the time? Why not me? Why did he have to continue going through pain? He had done nothing wrong but enter this world. I had so many whys for God. I'll admit some anger had built in me; then sudden sorrow washed over me for feeling angry. I just kept thinking of the story of Job again in the Bible—how everything was taken from him, and his questioning of the Lord—and again I felt, Who was I to ask why? Even though I sat in the room in a fetal position crying and crying, I began to recite over and over, "For when I am weak, You are strong; for when I am weak, You are strong; with God all things are possible"; and I remembered what Pastor Ken said, that God doesn't give you more than you can handle. I stood up thinking I must fight and be there for Noah, and I began to play worship music. I tried to gather what energy I had left to clean myself up and be ready to go back and see Noah. As I went on my way back to the NICU, I was in complete distress, trying to wrap my head around everything. Before buzzing into the NICU doors, I took a deep breath, prayed for comfort and peace, and walked in. When I got there, I heard a mother crying and crying, and a baby wailing as well. Once I entered, I saw him fast asleep. However, right across from me was the mother I had heard crying, along with her infant daughter. She stood over her bed and wept and wept. I felt so much sorrow for her. I wanted to hug her and say, "I know what you're going through, and I am here for you," but I stayed sitting by Noah, not because I wasn't concerned, but because I had been that mom and, most importantly, I didn't want anyone saying they understood what I was going through. I realized then there were others who were suffering around me. Each mom had her own story as to why she was here, and all I could do was look at the positive in my situation. My son was alive. Even though he needed help breathing, he was in a hospital where they provided the proper equipment for him, and most importantly, there was some hope of helping him to breathe on a machine and come home. That night I held Noah's hand and sang *"Mi papisito, mi chulito, mi Noahito, mi corazon, mi bebito, mi chulito, please don't take my sunshine away, please don't take my sunshine away."* He stayed asleep, and I was finally able to smile.

The next day, I began pumping at 3 a.m. and again at 6 a.m. I still wasn't making nearly enough to feed Noah for all his feedings, but at least for three feedings, he was getting my breast milk. I woke up feeling depressed, not because of Noah, but again because I couldn't pump what I was supposed to for him. Currently, I was doing everything possible—taking certain drops to increase milk production, eating oatmeal, snacking, lots of carbs, and a gallon of water. Still, nothing seemed to increase my milk production. As I arrived at the NICU to see Noah, there he was with his eyes open. I began singing to him and was able to complete the routine of suctioning him and changing his diaper. I was so afraid to change him. He was so tiny, and with him being my first baby, I was super delicate and fragile with him, trying to make sure I didn't disconnect any cords that were attached to him, which were his heart monitor, his pulse oximeter, his feeding tube, and his oxygen taped to his face. Shortly after, the social worker arrived and asked if I was ready for the meeting with all the specialists. I wanted to look and say no, but I figured I should put on a brave face and try to understand what was happening with my son. I retrieved a pen and a notebook, said a prayer, and walked into the conference room. In the conference room sat the pulmonologist, neonatal doctor, charge nurse of the NICU, resident doctor, social worker, and head doctor of the NICU. As I sat there with my pen and paper, I felt the weight of the world was on my shoulders. I smiled because I didn't know what else to do, whether this was going to be the best or worst day of life, or whether I was finally going to get an answer on my son's medical condition. Everyone went around the room and introduced themselves to me while all telling me how beautiful my little Noah was. The neonatal doctor began by going over and explaining Noah's Dandy Walker variant, which meant he had fluid in his brain that caused the cerebellum to split a bit and caused it to be smaller than normal. The doctor also stated that this might be causing Noah to desaturate and not able to breathe on his own, which was why they had him connected to oxygen twenty-four hours a day. The doctor stated that Noah was on a low dose of oxygen; however, the best outcome would be to wean him off oxygen so he would be able to breathe on room air. The pulmonologist began speaking and stated the sleep-study results had come back and determined that Noah was supposed to breathe thirty-two times a minute, but while he slept, he was only breathing eight times a minute. This meant that for some reason, possibly due to the split cerebellum, the brain was not stimulating and sending messages to the lungs to breathe. The doctor continued to state that this was known as central sleep apnea, but in its worst form. The pulmonologist also stated that Noah's lungs were strong, and he could breathe during the day while he was awake; however, while he slept, he didn't breathe. The doctor went on to state he would recommend a tracheostomy tube, where Noah could be connected to a ventilator 24/7 to prevent desaturations while he slept and to be able to breathe, unless he somehow started to breathe on his own in the upcoming days. My heart immediately sank, and I looked at everyone and asked, Would this be forever? Would his brain mature and stimulate? Would he have to be on a ventilator all his life? Why was this happening? Was this due to the fluid that was in his brain? The split cerebellum? The neonatal doctor looked at me with so much compassion and stated: "We don't know. We don't have a diagnosis, since the Dandy Walker variant is not attributed to respiratory issues. We believe there is another syndrome Noah has but are not sure which one, and we have a geneticist who is going to come to speak with you about a possible genetic disorder. I don't have any answers. The only thing I can tell you is we have to watch and observe him as he grows. The worst-case scenario is his brain doesn't stimulate and he is vent-dependent for the rest of his life. The best-case scenario is his brain matures and stimulates and he weans off the vent. However, we can't say which way this will go. We can only observe Noah and let him show us how this will play out." The doctor continued to state: "It would also be best for Noah to have a G-tube placed, since most babies with a trach find it uncomfortable to swallow. To prevent any issues with his nutrition and growth, it is best to have the G-tube placement surgery the same day as the tracheostomy to prevent having two surgery dates." The pulmonologist began to state: "Before we can proceed with the surgery, Noah will need to gain eight pounds, which he is currently at seven. Then afterward, in order for you to take him home, you would need two months of training so you could become familiar with how to take care of Noah with a trach. Also, he will have to gain ten pounds in order to be transferred to a home ventilator, since that is the minimum weight requirement that is needed." The doctor continued to state: "Also, it depends on whether or not Noah does better with his desaturations. We will not send him home if he continues to have desaturations, since we wouldn't want to put him at risk and you in any negative position." My eyes immediately began to water, and all I could think about was my poor son. He had done nothing to deserve this; he just entered this world, and yet he would have to go through extreme pain. There was nothing I could do as his mother to help him, or even to say everything was going to be okay. I thought, *Why him? What did he do to deserve this?* This world was supposed to be a beautiful, happy place for him, and now it seemed as if he had entered a world full of pain and torment, and we had no idea when this was going to end. I began to think of Mary, Jesus's mother, the way she must have felt when her son Jesus was tortured and killed, how she stood looking at Him and wept. I could imagine the pain she must have felt when she couldn't help her son and all she could do was watch and pray for some peace, and hope the suffering would end. I wondered if she felt like me, how unfair it was that her son was experiencing so much agony, how she couldn't stop it, and how she would give anything in the world to switch places with Him. I kept my composure, even though I wanted to scream and cry and go into a fetal position and beg God to please allow me to go through the pain and suffering instead of Noah. I mustered up the words to finally speak and asked, "How long are you giving him to breathe on his own before we proceed with the surgery?" The neonatal doctor responded, "Two weeks, and let's hope for a miracle." I agreed, and even though I was broken inside, I kept thinking, *Thank God I believe in a God who performs miracles.*

October 7 (Day 1 of Two Weeks)

The next morning, I woke up and refused to have any negative thoughts. I turned on my worship music, where I heard "Another in the Fire," "Whole Heart," and "You Make Me Brave." I created a playlist for myself so it would constantly be on repeat. I began to pray in the shower and beg God to let Noah breathe on his own. I recited, "In the name of Jesus, let Noah's brain somehow stimulate on its own." I'll even admit that even though I knew it was absolutely wrong to do, I pleaded and begged for Him to give me Noah's condition and make him healthy. I went downstairs to the diner and made oatmeal to try to increase my milk production and told myself, *Today I am going to do skin-to-skin and do whatever I can to help Noah.* I ordered a shuttle to the hospital, and while waiting on the stairs, I became so emotional and couldn't believe this had become my life. I went from living in a loving two-bedroom apartment in a small town with my fiancé to now living at a Ronald McDonald House two hours away from my home in a big city. I went from being so happy my baby was on the way to now horrified at what would happen to Noah, and whether or not we would be going home. As soon as the shuttle came, I wiped my tears. The driver approached me and asked if I was going to Kaiser. I stated yes, and he opened the door for me and asked me how my day was. I sat down, and he began conversing with me about the city and about his day. I began telling him what part of LA I grew up in, and he mentioned to me where I could find the best tacos in LA. As soon as we got to Kaiser, he opened the door for me and told me to have a great day. I got off the shuttle, forgetting about the negativity in my head, and thought how one person, who probably thought nothing of it, could be your angel in disguise, not knowing how much importance they had on your day to make you feel somewhat better, though they thought they were just carrying out a normal, typical day and conversation. As of today, I wish I would have gotten his name to reach out and thank him, but I only thanked the main powerful source I could, and that was Jesus Christ, my Savior. As I entered the hospital, I was very optimistic, hoping that I would hear some good news and hoping Noah had not had desaturation episodes throughout the night. Once I arrived there, I met with Noah's nurse for the day, and she gave me information on what had happened throughout the night. She told me Noah had fifteen desaturations and had to be bagged twice (where a CPR bag had to be placed on his trach for compressions to start). Also, he had been good with no crying episodes and seemed to be growing and gaining weight slowly. I stood over Noah's crib and grabbed his hand. I told him, "Momma's here," and asked how he was as he lay there asleep. I put my hand on his head and began to pray in the name of Jesus: "Please stimulate Noah's brain. Please allow him to breathe on his own, and please heal him. I love You and thank You, Father. I ask all this in the name of Your Son, Jesus Christ. Amen." As I opened my eyes, I felt much better, despite hearing the news about Noah. I sat there with him next to his crib, and at 8 a.m., I was finally able to change his diaper and do the daily routine of checking his temperature with the thermometer under his armpit. I finally began to learn Noah's baseline temperature. He was always at ninety-eight degrees, and I learned that he was always hot. Just from being swaddled, he would sweat up a storm, and it didn't help that he had a head full of hair, just like me when I was a baby. I was so delicate with him; I didn't know any better. Luckily, I had a great nurse who showed me how to correctly change a diaper. As they set up his morning feeding, I asked if I could hold him for the hour. The nurse asked me if I wanted to try to bottle-feed him, since he was up to five milliliters of bottle-feeding. I was so excited. Finally, I would get to bottle-feed my baby and feel some normalcy. I was a first-time mom and no idea how to feed a baby. I slowly placed Noah in my arms and slightly placed the bottle in his mouth. I waited patiently for him to try to latch on to the nipple. Once he latched, he started to suck the nipple so fast that he began choking. I sat him up, afraid his vitals would drop. I was constantly looking at the monitor, so afraid I would do something to cause a desaturation. The nurse noticed my nervousness and came over to show me how to feed Noah. She tried to feed him as I did, but soon after, he began choking again. She placed him in her lap and sat him in an angled position and tried to feed him again. Once he sat in that position, he was able to take in the milk and was able to do the suck-and-swallow motion without choking or spitting up. I began to ask why he was doing that. The nurse mentioned that he didn't have the suck-and-swallow motion down pat yet, which might be why he was choking. She handed him to me, and I placed him on my lap and mimicked how the nurse had positioned Noah and the bottle. As soon as I did this, Noah was able to latch on to the bottle. He finished the last of his five milliliters, and I held him to burp him. Once he burped, my eyes teared up. It was such an emotional process for me. Here I was, finally feeding my baby, holding him in my arms to burp him, making me feel somewhat normal despite all this. I tried my best not to cry and thought about how grateful I was to be able to feed my son. It's amazing how sometimes it's the little things we take for granted. However, for me in that moment, feeding my son was everything to me, and I thanked God for giving me that moment. The nurse was able to set up his feed while I held him in my arms.

I began to rock him and sing "You Are My Sunshine"; in that moment, I felt his little hand reach for my chest, and his eyes opened and he was just staring at me. I imagined what he was thinking or possibly feeling. He was looking up at me as if stating, "Mom, you're here. Is it really you?" He continued to stare at me and I continued to sing. At this point, I couldn't contain my emotions and I silently cried. I didn't know what else do. I felt as if I wanted to tell him so much to make him understand why I couldn't be there all the time. I just held my tears and told him how sorry I was. I was sorry for not being there all the time, sorry this was happening, sorry if he felt alone, and sorry for not being able to produce enough milk to feed him. I held him so tight and continued to sing and tried my best to wipe the sadness and guilt away. I wasn't going to let it ruin our victorious moment, no matter how small it was. I focused on the positive, being able to feed him. This little victory made me think positive. I began telling Noah how strong he was, and how God was here with him when I was not, and to look for the angels as they slept in his crib, and told him how they watched over him. I hugged him and kissed his head, and from there I sat in complete happiness with my son in my arms. This was all I wanted, so I took all the victories I could get.

At 12 p.m., I left to go eat lunch in the cafeteria, since the NICU closed for two hours in order for the doctors to do rounds with the nurses. As I walked the long hallway, I noticed the same employees there in the cafeteria. I felt at this point the cooks knew me by now; I was having either a pepperoni pizza or a bacon cheeseburger. The workers saw me there every day for lunch, breakfast, and sometimes dinner, so they began to give me a staff discount. The coffee-bean staff member even began to give me a large caramel Frappuccino instead of the small one I ordered. I don't know if they felt sorry for me, or the expression on my face said it all. Regardless, I was grateful. Any little way people helped, I greatly appreciated it. At this point, funds were low, and I was going to have to start getting the donated food from the Ronald McDonald House. We had no income coming in, and unfortunately, my fiancé wasn't working at the time in order to be there for Noah. I hated asking for money. Yes, it was my pride, but also, I was embarrassed that I was at the lowest point of my life and needed all the help I could get. I reached out to my family, asking for help, and I thanked God for them every day. They were my support system and helped us financially.

While sitting deep in thought in the cafeteria, I started to look around and saw some of the NICU moms in the cafeteria. There was one mom in particular whose daughter was right next to Noah. I saw her by herself eating and wondered what she was going through. I never saw anyone with her; she was always by herself, always there with her daughter. I sympathized with her so much. I didn't know if she was alone or what her story was, but we always seemed to nod to each other as though we were both aware of each other's pain. I wanted to approach her so badly just to say hello, to say that I was here if she wanted to talk, but I stopped myself. I knew if I talked to her, I would probably just break down and cry because for once there would be someone experiencing the same pain as I was, and for once I would feel as if I wasn't alone. As I walked back toward the elevators, I nodded my head in her direction and smiled at her; she gave me a nod and smiled back.

I entered the fourth floor for what felt like the hundredth time, I buzzed to go inside and did the normal routine of getting a locker to put my stuff in, since they advised us not to take any items into the room due to bacteria and high-risk babies. As I walked towards pod G, I heard a commotion of machines going off, respiratory therapists running in. I ran in, knowing something was wrong. There were five people around Noah's bed, and all I could do was watch. One nurse was holding him in an upright position as he became purple, while another was bagging him with a CPR bag and raising the oxygen level. The respiratory therapist was connecting the hospital ventilator to a tube that was connected to Noah's oxygen line. All this was happening at such a quick pace that all I could focus on was the monitor beeping and seeing Noah's oxygen levels drop to fifty, forty-five, thirty-four, twenty-three, all while his heart rate was down to sixty, and all I could do was stand from afar and watch this unravel. All I could do was think, *Not my baby. Please, Lord, let him breathe.* I secretly cheered him on, just repeating in my head, *Please breathe, Noah.* As soon as the hospital ventilator was connected to Noah's oxygen line, his heart rate and oxygen level shot up and he was now stable. The nurse placed him back on the bed and swaddled Noah on his side to relax. She walked over and informed me that Noah had clamped down and held his breath when he became upset, causing the oxygen line (via nose) not to be fully forced into his lungs, which was why they were hooking him up to the hospital ventilator that would apply more pressure so the air would go more quickly into his lungs. The respiratory therapist walked over to me and showed me the hospital ventilator and stated that Noah was getting 8 percent oxygen, and informed me that the oxygen from the mask was not enough for him. As the commotion settled down, I walked over to his crib and looked down at Noah, placed my hand on his head, and began praying: "Lord, you know my heart, what I am feeling. I don't have the words right now, but please heal my son and stimulate his brain. Please, I beg of You, help us. Be with him when I am not. Let him see Your presence and know he is not alone. I ask all this in the name of Your Son, Jesus Christ. Amen." Once I opened my eyes, I saw Noah peeking to see who was there. I smiled at him and told him how much I loved him and how sorry I was for not being there when the desaturation happened. I just wanted to hold my son, to comfort him, to tell him Momma was here and he was going to be okay. However, I couldn't; all I could do was look at him in his bed and hold his hand. Noah had three leads placed on his chest, with wires leading to a box connector on the side of his feet. He had a pulse-oximeter wire placed around his foot, with a bandage wrapped over it to hold the sensor in place. He had a feeding tube placed in his nose that also led to the side by his feet area. He also had an oxygen-wire hose to his nose, with tape wrapped on his cheeks to hold it into place. His skin was so sensitive from the tape that was placed on his face that he constantly had red cheeks. He also had an oxygen tube placed in his nose that led to a hospital ventilator machine, which was now placed right next to his hospital crib. As I stood placing my finger in his hand and rubbing his hand, I began to sing "You Are My Sunshine," so he would know Momma was there. As I sang, my eyes watered. I was looking at my son full of wires, thinking how he had to be bagged, and as his mother, there was absolutely nothing I could do for him. I felt weak, and all I could do was hold a brave face and recite the Bible verse "For when I am weak, You are strong" over and over. Internally, I wanted to collapse and just cry due to what I had just witnessed, knowing that this incident was showing he was still not breathing correctly on his own and we had only two weeks to get him there. The doctor walked in shortly afterward and informed me this was the second time Noah had to be bagged even though he was getting oxygen through his nose. They felt because he got upset and clamped down, he stopped the air from going into his lungs, which caused him to turn purple and desaturate. The doctor felt the hospital ventilator would be stronger, since it was a stronger force and pressure of air being pushed into Noah's airway. The doctor also mentioned they were giving him a bit of oxygen to help him recover, but eventually they wanted to wean him off the oxygen just to room air, since he was originally on that before he started desaturating back-to-back. He expressed to me that Noah was okay and that all we could do was try to prevent him from clamping down and holding his breath, but tomorrow they would check in to see how he was doing with the hospital ventilator. All I could do was just nod and smile and say thank you. As I sat there holding Noah's hand, I noticed he was fast asleep. No matter how many times I saw Noah turn fully purple, it was something I couldn't adjust to. It scared me each and every time, not knowing if this was it, if this was going to be the time that he stayed purple and didn't come back, or if this was going to be the time when he lost so much oxygen for a period of time that he was now brain dead. I would always whisper to Noah, "You are going to be okay," and that God was there watching over him, and to keep strong and keep on fighting. I would try to explain to him that this wasn't how life was supposed to be. It was not all pain and misery; there was also love and happiness. Soon he would get to experience this, but he had to keep fighting. As 4 p.m. turned to 8 p.m., I knew I had to go eat and get some rest, even though I didn't want to. I stood up, and as I said good-bye to Noah, I grabbed every strand of strength I could and walked out of the area, leaving my son behind. I felt so guilty. How I wished I could just stay with him and comfort him, let him know someone was there watching over him. But all I could do was walk away and cry. I held back my emotions as I left the NICU; I did not want to be seen crying. But as I heard the door shut behind me from the NICU, I ran straight to the restroom, closed the stall, and cried like a baby. I didn't want to eat or sleep, but I knew if I couldn't be healthy for Noah, who would be there? I had to take care of myself and eat and sleep, even if that meant having to walk away for the night. It was the hardest thing a mother could do, especially while their child was in need, and I would never wish that pain and guilt and sadness on anyone. It is something I wish no parent will ever have to feel.

Day 7 of Two Weeks

A week went by, and I did the same routine: I woke up at 5 a.m., showered, went downstairs to eat breakfast, and then grabbed my bags, breast pump, and snacks for the day. I would pump for twenty-five minutes, then store the milk in a container and call for a shuttle. I would usually arrive at the NICU by 9 a.m. and meet with the nurse to discuss what had occurred overnight, how many desaturations Noah had and whether any changes had been made. When I arrived, Noah had a new nurse, since they did a five-day rotation. I wish I remembered her name; she was very friendly, and I could tell she truly cared about the infants in the NICU. She told me that Noah had multiple desaturations but did not have to be bagged, which was a good thing. She also informed me that I could bring clothes for Noah so he wouldn't have to wear the hospital clothes. I told her I didn't know we could do so, and she stated yes, we could bring whatever we wanted for the baby and leave it underneath his crib, even books and music too. I was instantly happy. I had thought we couldn't do anything like that, since we were in a crowded room with other parents and because of the restrictions they had in the NICU. Luckily, I had clothes from the time when I packed Noah's backpack on the delivery date. The nurse told me she would be right back to help me do skin-to-skin with Noah. I was amazed; for the first time, I had someone warm and caring who already knew exactly what I wanted and what Noah needed. She came in with a nice, comforting reclining chair and closed the curtains so I could be shirtless with my son. As soon as I was ready, she came in and placed all his cords neatly in his swaddled blanket and handed him to me. She closed the curtain and told me to call for her when I was done or tired. I finally got the privacy I craved and longed for, since it had been chaos for the past three weeks. There was no one staring, no one interfering with our bonding time—just Noah and I closed off to the world. I held him to my chest and sang "You Are My Sunshine." Immediately he opened his eyes. I began asking him how he was and what he was dreaming about. I began to tell him how sorry I was, and that he was going to be okay, and we would be home soon. I started to talk to him about God. I told him how I thought Jesus looked, and let Noah know that if he saw Him, He was his friend and his protector. I told him to look for the angels flying around his bed and know they were there to play with him and protect him. I talked to him about me and who I was and my childhood, and how I hoped he would enjoy some of the stuff I did as a kid, like playing sports and riding a bike. I talked and talked. I felt as though time had frozen and nothing could interfere—no health issues, no nothing—just my son and I, something I had hoped and prayed for, for at least ten years. The nurse entered the curtain and told me it was time for Noah to eat again, so we hooked up his feed and I held him for another hour. The doctor knocked and came in and asked if she could speak with me afterward, and I told her of course. Once Noah's feed was over, the nurse called for the doctor, and she came five minutes later and asked how I was doing. I told her I was good but more worried about Noah. I also began to lay everything on her and express that I needed answers to prepare for what was to come. Would Noah's brain ever stimulate? Would his motor skills be affected? Would he ever have a normal life? Could he outgrow the trach? What was going on? The doctor told me she didn't have the answers for me, that she wished she could tell me what was going to happen. She handed me a packet about tracheostomy and gastrostomy tubes, which included information as well as a DVD showing how it was to have a trach baby and what care I would have to provide for Noah. I was a bit confused as to why she gave me a G-tube packet. I knew exactly what a G-tube was; I was very familiar with it, since I had a cousin with a G-tube and had taken care of him. I looked at her puzzled and asked if this packet was for me. She stated, "Yes. That is what I am here to discuss with you." She began to inform me that it would be best for Noah to have a G-tube placed as well, since he was having issues with swallowing. She informed me some babies do not like to swallow after a trach is placed, which can lead to other issues if they are not getting the proper nutrition. I knew Noah was having trouble swallowing, but I had been so focused on him not breathing that the fact of him eating or not was on the back burner in my mind. However, after realizing a G-tube was being placed, I began to see how serious this might be. I asked her, "Does this have anything to do with his swallow test?" and she said yes. The results of his swallow test revealed that he did pass it, but for some reason, the liquid would sit on the flap tissue called the epiglottis (this flap prevents going food into the lungs) instead of going straight down to his stomach. She stated he technically passed, but they didn't know why he wouldn't swallow fully. She said the G-tube would be a precautionary factor, that they would still try to feed him and get him off the G-tube, but they just wanted to make sure he continued to eat and grow, especially since he would have to gain a total of ten pounds before he could leave the hospital. I nodded, smiled, and she said, "Read the information. Take time to go over it, and I'll check in tomorrow with you to see if you have any questions or concerns." I didn't know how to take in the information; it wasn't something I wanted to hear. My son was yet again going to have another surgery, be in pain, have to recover from two parts of his body, and he wasn't even a month old. There was nothing I could do to take away the pain, and I had to sign the paperwork indicating I approved both surgeries. I wanted to break down and cry again. How could I be strong hearing this news when mentally and psychically I was broken and bruised? I felt as though I couldn't win, and the hardest part of all was as a mother, I wanted to protect my child from pain and trauma because I saw what would come, what were the side effects, and yet there was nothing I could do. I felt it was so unfair again, and I began questioning everything once more. Why him? What did Noah ever do? Why not me? I began to question whether he felt as if this is what it meant to be in the world—full of hurt, pain, sadness, and loneliness. He was a baby who should be feeling happiness, comfort, safety, and the warmth of his family around, but he was only allowed to see two people at a time for only a certain amount of time. Every day he fought for his life to breathe, having tubes and wires in his nose, mouth, chest, and feet. How was this fair? He hadn't even sinned in life, and yet he was being exposed to pain. Again I sympathized with Mary, having to think my son had done nothing wrong but was being treated this way, and there was nothing I could do but pray and hope he didn't suffer anymore. I wished I was strong like her; she was able to stand by the cross as He took his final breaths, and yet here I was, wanting to run away from it all and it hadn't even begun yet. Everyone told me God only gives you things you can endure, and even though I know it was wrong to say, my response was, "I wish He viewed me as weak so I wouldn't have to take on circumstances like this." For the first time, I didn't think I would be strong enough to take this on. I had had things happen to me in my life, to which my response had always been to bring it on; I could overcome it because I knew how strong I was. But when it is happening to your child and there is nothing you can do, you feel so helpless, weak, and, most of all, in agony. I didn't want Noah to feel everything I was feeling, so I decided to leave the NICU and go have lunch at the Ronald McDonald House. I took a shuttle back to the house and sat and waited while a church congregation came and prepared us food. I was so tired from crying; it had put so much exhaustion on my body, so I just sat there trying to become numb, silently praying for God to heal me and make me strong.

After lunch I went outside to take a walk. I felt choked up inside, as though there were knots in my throat. As I saw couples holding hands or people walking their dogs, I would think how they could be so happy, how lucky they were to feel happiness and the joy of the world; meanwhile, I felt my life was crumbling and falling apart. As I finished, I decided to go back to the room to try to gather myself because at this point, I was not seeing the positive of anything. As soon as I entered the room, it was like a ton of bricks hit me. All the emotion and pain I was feeling hit me, and I just lay there again in a fetal position, crying and crying. It felt like forever, but when I looked at the time, one hour had passed. I kept telling myself to get up and fight. Noah needed me there; he didn't need me breaking down and thinking the worst of the worst. After the fifth time of telling myself to get up, I rose to my feet, put on worship music, which was the Hillsong worship song "Whole Heart," and began singing. I felt that was the only thing I could do, just sing my heart out, and that's what I did. I sat on the bed and sang. After the song was over, I hopped in the shower, got ready, and put Visine in my eyes to clear up the redness. I began to speak light and positivity in my life and said, "God, You are here. I know I'm not alone, and I know You are protecting my son. He has a purpose in life, whether it is to have a strong testimony about what he encountered at a young age, or whether it is to make him strong. I know God's hand is in this, and He is here." I got ready and went back to the NICU. Noah was awake, just staring at the ceiling. I was so happy to see him with his eyes open and looking around as if he was finally curious to see what was going on, what all the commotion was about with all the beeping machines and chatter from the hospital staff. I leaned over his crib and started saying, "Hi, papisito. It's Momma." He smiled, and my heart immediately melted and felt warm. Noah was a happy boy; despite everything, he was smiling. I kept singing to him over and over, and I remembered all the childhood songs my mom sang to me. I began to play those songs for him: "Old McDonald," "Green Grass Grows All Around," and "Bingo." He was curious about the music playing. I kept clapping my hands while singing, and Noah began smiling and smiling. It was then that I learned how much he loved music. The nurse heard him laughing and walked over. She began to tell me that I could always bring stuff from home for him, such as books, music, clothes, stuffed animals, and blankets. I got so excited because I still had his diaper bag with me that had everything, including toys and a stuffed animal. I left his stuffed animal by his crib and placed his clothes nearby, and the nurse told me she would put on his clothes after he ate. As the time drifted into dinnertime, I was getting ready to leave for shift change so I could pick up food for myself, so I started saying my good-bye prayers with Noah and telling him I would be back after shift change at eight to say good night. Even though it was going on three weeks of being in the hospital, I still was not used to telling him good-bye and leaving him there. I felt so empty and numb, as though my heart was being ripped out each time I left because I didn't have my baby with me. I closed my eyes, kissed his forehead, and walked out as fast as I could, my eyes watery, praying that he didn't feel me leave, praying that he didn't feel alone. That night I walked to a taco stand and ordered tacos. I didn't want to return to the Ronald McDonald House because I knew once I lay down, I wasn't going to get up. I ordered food and sat outside at a nearby table, next to a couple who were laughing and joking. Everyone seemed in the Halloween spirit. There were people walking throughout Hollywood with bags of Halloween decorations, and the couple next to me were talking about their costume selections. That's when it hit me like a ton of bricks, that Noah wasn't going to enjoy his first Halloween. He wasn't going to see the apartment I had decorated for him, and he wasn't going to be enjoying the Dumbo costume we had bought for him to wear. Even though I was trying to remain positive, I couldn't help but think we were more than likely going to be in the hospital for Halloween, and even though we said to be positive, I knew in my heart we would still be in the hospital, surgery or not.

October 11, 2019 (Two Weeks)

The day came when we would find out whether Noah would be able to go home on oxygen or needed the trach surgery along with G-tube surgery. I walked in hopeful, praying for some good news, hoping for a miracle. As I entered the elevator to go to the fourth floor to the NICU, I kept reciting in my head, *My God can move mountains.* I entered Noah's pod G, and I arrived right when the doctors were making rounds. The neonatal doctor came and asked me how I was doing. I informed her, "I am good, hopeful for today's news." The doctor smiled at me and said, "Noah's desaturations are the same, and we would like to recommend both surgeries." My heart sank. The more I knew that the surgery was inevitable, the more I didn't want to accept it. I had been hoping for the best outcome that I didn't even think about how I would feel about the decision to do surgery or even if I wanted to sign the paperwork and consent to it. As my eyes started to swell and get watery, I looked at the doctor and asked her a simple question: "Will this allow Noah to not fight to breathe anymore?" Once she said, "Yes, it will help him breathe," I knew I had to do it, even though every bone in my body wanted to say no. The doctor looked at me and stated for me to go take a break from the NICU, and she gave me encouraging advice. She told me I had to take care of myself, that she knew how it was hard for me, but I must continue my life and be the best I could be for Noah. Just then the charge nurse, Ellen, arrived and began saying hi to Noah while the doctor talked to me. Nurse Ellen chimed in and started to tell me that I was there all the time and needed to get out to go take a breather. She told me Noah was in the best care and place he could possibly be right now. I knew this was all true; in a short amount of time, I had managed to sleep only two to three hours a night, hardly ate, and was worried 24/7. However, it was something I wrestled with internally. How could I go out and enjoy anything, whether it was a walk, a warm meal, or even visiting family, when my son was in the hospital by himself? How was that enjoying myself? When I was out, I was just thinking about my son, if he was okay and whether he felt alone. How can any mother truly say she feels okay to leave her baby's hospital bed and not feel guilty about it? I don't think any mother can do it, and if they do, I'm sure they wear a smile on their face but deep down inside feel as if they are being stabbed in the heart and a part of them is missing. I don't think people understand an ounce of what NICU moms go through. That is not to say a NICU mom's pain is more severe than others, but it is truly different and unique. Think of it: We go from carrying our child for nine months in our womb, we feel every kick and flutter movement, we talk to our child, we read to our child, we feel their very presence every day. Then the baby leaves the womb, and instead of taking them into our arms against our chest every night as it's supposed to happen, we leave them in a hospital pod, where we are left to only grab their little hand, spend only a few hours with them, and afterward leave to go back to an empty bed where our child is not with us all the time. We fantasize for nine months about all the things we will be doing with our child, all the great memories, the places to take them, and activities to do. Then *bam*—we realize it's not going to happen that way and have no idea what's in store for us and our baby. So now we must grieve all that we planned and fantasized about. How do you say, "Okay, that's fine," or "Okay, let me go try to be happy"? Yes, I understood it was for my well-being, but I would be lying if I said I could fully leave my son in the hospital, go out to get fresh air, and be okay about it. I guess the charge nurse noticed that my mind was elsewhere thinking other thoughts while she was telling me this and trying to give me helpful advice, because she placed her hands on my shoulders and looked me in the eye and said, "Natalie, you need to be the best version of yourself for Noah. If you are not okay and healthy, who will come and watch him? Who will be there for Noah? He will need his mom, and what happens if you don't feel well enough? Noah has only one mom, so please leave and go get some rest." Right when she said that, it was like a truck hit me. How could I have been so selfish? How could I have doubted my faith? This is where I needed my faith to kick in and give it to the Lord so that I could build myself. I needed to do as I said and trust God to be there and watch my son when I couldn't. I needed to trust God to make things better for both Noah and me. Even though I said God was here with me, I had been walking this path alone, trying to take on the world, when I had Jesus here right along with me, wanting to carry the load for me. I looked at the nurse and told her, "You're right," and kissed Noah and stood up and left. As I walked out, I cried. No matter how many times I did this walk, I cried. This was a harder cry, however, because for once I knew I wasn't alone. God was here with me to help, to be my comfort, my support, and, most of all, my Savior. I went to the Ronald McDonald House searching for God any way I could. I read the verse of the day. I opened the Highlands app (the local church I attended) and listened to last week's message. I did whatever I could possibly do to hear God's Word, to feel His presence and know He was there. My phone vibrated, and a text message came in from my uncle. He sent me just one thing: Hebrews 11:7. I immediately looked up the verse to see what it said and it read like this: "By faith, Noah built a ship in the middle of dry land. He was warned about something he couldn't see and acted on what he was told. The result? His family was saved. His act of faith drew a sharp line between the evil of the unbelieving world and the rightness of the believing world. As a result, Noah became intimate with God" (MSG). I knew then that this was the motivation, or sign, as you might say, to know God had been with me all along. Even though my little Noah was going to face hard times, he could overcome it and live in faith with God. I cried and cried; God was here, and now I knew what I had to do. I had to put on the armor of God, face my fears, and help my son with whatever support and love that I could as we embarked on this journey. I called my sister-in-law, who was an RN, to go over the doctor jargon. I knew what was happening with my son, but I needed more reassurance in layman's terms. She went over with me what a tracheotomy was, how it would benefit Noah, and of course the territory it came with. She was the only one I trusted; I felt she understood my pain to some degree, since she also had had her boys in the NICU. Once she explained everything to me on how a tracheostomy worked and what new changes would come, I felt more at ease. I had always been a person to want to know what I was facing so I could have a direct plan of action and know how to tackle what lay ahead. I asked her one simple thing, and it was my greatest fear of all: What if I couldn't do it? What if it was too much for me? I never wanted to admit it, but on top of everything I was going through, I was so scared that I wouldn't be strong enough to take care of my son outside of the hospital, and I didn't want to fail my son. She then reminded me that God gave me this gift and knew what was going to happen, and He picked the strongest woman for the task. It gave me a beacon of hope, knowing that she was right. God gives you what you can handle, and I needed to continue to trust Him to be there every step of the way.

I told her the news of everything that had taken place, from the decision to the surgery to even getting a surgery date of October 16, 2019, which was five days from now. As much as I wanted to grieve because I felt the battle was lost, I had to remind myself again that the war was not over and I would be victorious in it. After the phone call, I wanted to escape and not think of my current situation. I wanted to pretend just for a few hours that this wasn't my life. Noah's dad agreed we should go out and try to continue our life. We needed to do our best to not forget about us. Even though we were dealing with something traumatic with our newborn son, we needed to remember the love we had and stick through it. I did my best to try to get ready. It was the first time I had put on makeup or even attempted to dress up. It took every ounce of strength in me to change. It was then I realized how much my body had changed as a woman. My jeans no longer fit my hips, my shirts were snug around my stomach area, and the stretch marks and C-section scar were visible and formed a pouch. I kept thinking to myself, *What am I doing? How can I be going out to eat, with my son in the hospital alone?* I had to keep shrugging off the thoughts because I knew if I gave in to them, I wouldn't go and I would go straight back to the hospital. Once I entered the car, as we were headed to go eat dinner, my eyes became teary as we passed the hospital, knowing Noah was in there without us, and I broke. I began crying and crying, telling my fiancé how guilty I felt as a mother for not being there with Noah, how unhappy I was. He grabbed my hand and told me to let it out, and I did, until it felt as though I had no more tears. I felt better, as if I had been holding in everything, trying to be strong, trying not to break, and, most importantly, by talking to someone who was going through the exact same pain and torture I was. We ended up going to Johnny Rocket's, and I splurged. I had a cheeseburger, fries, a shake, and a coke. We ended up talking about other things besides our situation, like being in LA and trying to make the most of it, how the city had grown on us, and how much we missed home. We walked around CityWalk and looked in different stores and just pretended we were out on a date. It felt good to be out; I felt I could finally take a long, deep breath. However, as much as I wanted to shake the thoughts and feelings, Noah was still on the back of my mind. I would drift off in a daydream, wondering what nurse was watching him and whether or not he was okay. I began praying, *Lord, please be there with him. Let him know Your presence. Let him see the angels. Make it known You are there and he is not alone.* As badly as I didn't want to say it, I was happy once we were done with dinner and it was time to go home, because I knew I could head back and be able to tell Noah good night. Once we were in the car, I asked my fiancé if we could stop by the hospital to wish Noah good night. We arrived at the hospital and did that long, lonely walk from the parking lot to inside the building. The security knew us by now, so it didn't matter whether we had our badge on or not. Once we got upstairs, I was so excited to see him. Even though it would be hard for me to say good-bye, it gave me a form of peace to be able to tell him good night. Once we entered the NICU, we saw Noah just staring at the ceiling. I began to call his name and grab his hand, and he smiled a bit. I told him how much we missed him, and that I had brought books to leave by his crib so I could read to him. I had two books with me that I had always forgotten to bring for Noah, and finally I brought them and placed them next to his crib. Every day while I was pregnant, I would read *Jesus Always*, a daily devotional, and *I Will Love You Forever* (*Te Amaré por Siempre*). I began to read him these books, and he continued to keep his eyes open and looked around as if he remembered the words. My eyes instantly began to water once I saw him smiling while I was reading *I Will Love You Forever*. Even though he was my son, I always held on to that guilt of not being able to be there for him in the beginning and to breastfeed him. I always wondered if he truly knew I was his mom, especially since I didn't get to spend the first few days of his life with him. My family would say of course he knew me, but it was the guilt that was deep in me that brought these thoughts to my mind. Once I began to read the devotional, he began to smile. Just that smile was the reassurance I needed to know that my son did have a bond with me and, as dumb as it sounds, wasn't feeling neglected by me. I smiled and praised God because I knew He continued to give me signs that everything was going to be okay, no matter how much the enemy wanted me to believe it wasn't. After reading to him, we helped the nurse change his diaper and do his temperature check, as well as rotate him from his position so he wouldn't be lying in only one position. Once 11 p.m. hit, I told Noah good night and said I would be there first thing in the morning to see him. As I walked away, it was a bittersweet moment. Yes, I was leaving my son, but for once I felt I could do this.

October 14, 2019

As I walked into the NICU bright and early, I knew today was the day I had to sign the paperwork to do both surgeries, the day I would speak with the surgeons to go over what was to come. I headed to Noah's pod and saw the doctors were already there discussing Noah's case with the nurses and specialists. Each specialist introduced himself: the head-and-neck doctor, Dr. N. and the gastroenterologist for the G-tube. The ENT discussed with me that the surgeries would be taking place around 9 a.m., but they would take Noah at 8 a.m. for the prep. The trach surgery would last an hour, and he would have stitches for a few days and be swollen for a couple of days. She explained to me that once he had his trach, the tape and oxygen line across his nose would be removed and he would be hooked to the hospital ventilator. The gastroenterologist stepped in and said the G-tube was usually a fast surgery and would be done first. The doctor expressed that they would be going through the belly button to insert the G-tube, and gauze would be placed around the G-tube to help with the swelling and bleeding. They both told me it shouldn't be more than two hours for the surgeries, and afterward Noah would be placed in recovery for another hour. Then they would transfer him back to the NICU, where we would be able to see him and be with him. I just smiled and nodded, knowing inside I was terrified. I signed the paperwork and shoved all my feelings aside and just held my son. Noah's nurse for the day asked me if I wanted to do skin-to-skin with him, and I said yes. She also told me to try to get as many hours as I could to hold him because usually after the surgery, they gave the baby a few days to recover before they started moving him in and out of the bed. I just took what she said and put it on the back burner; I didn't want anything to ruin the time I was about to have with him. I held him for four hours doing skin-to-skin, playing Christian lullabies, and singing to him. Every three and a half hours, I would grab my bag from the locker that contained my breast pump and go to the breast-pumping room to try my best to produce something for Noah. Then it was a process of cleaning the pump, putting the breast milk in a bag, and labeling it with the hospital tags, writing the date and time it was pumped. From there it was handed to the nurse to be used or placed in the refrigerator for the next feeding. This was done around the clock, no matter where I was, in order to try to increase my milk production. After each pumping, I would become so tired, but I tried to do my best to eat and to drink water for energy. I felt all the urgency in the world to give him as much breast milk as I could, especially since he was going to be recovering from his surgeries soon. After pumping, I went to check on Noah and saw he was asleep, so I headed down to the cafeteria for lunch until the NICU reopened at 4 p.m. For a straight week, I ordered the same dish: a bacon cheeseburger, curly fries, and a Coke Zero. The cafeteria workers knew me by now, so I continued to receive a staff discount. While eating, I sent a group to text to my family, telling them the news: Noah would be having surgery that Friday, October 18, 2019, and if they could, please pray for us. I felt I needed all the prayers I could get, so I reached out to my friends on social media and asked for prayers as well. My biggest struggle had always been discussing my feelings and emotions when I was going through something. For weeks, I wanted to call Debbie, who was a fellow Christian who led a women's Bible study group I had frequently attended in the past, but I didn't know what to say. I wanted to say "Help" and just emotionally vomit on her, because she was the only person I felt safe with. However, I was so ashamed about my stance with God, about my lack of faith, that I felt embarrassed to call myself a Christian, especially when I was struggling with my hope and faith, and questioning God. I grabbed a coffee and began contemplating what to say or even if I should text her. Finally, I gave in. I felt I had nothing to lose; it was time to put down my walls and not stand alone in this battle. I thought of the verse that two are better than one when going through something. I grabbed my phone and simply wrote: "Hi, Debbie. Just wanted to let you know my son was born on 9/27/19. I have been in the hospital ever since, and he will be going through surgery this Friday for a tracheostomy and a G-tube placement. If you could please pray for us and ask the ladies in the Bible study group to pray for us as well, thank you so much. Hope all is well, and please say hello to your mother for me." I instantly received a reply back, and she told me she hoped I was doing well and did not know I had been in the hospital. She said she would like to visit soon to meet my son, and she wanted me to know that she was here for me and praying, and would inform the ladies to pray for Noah too. She told me how strong I was and not to forget God was with me, and that she loved me, and to let her know when she could drop by. I told her it would be best on the weekend, and she told me to let her know and she would be there. I felt relieved. I had my family with me, of course, who were my emotional support system, but I always felt I had to hold myself together. I didn't want to show anyone how broken, bruised, and mentally exhausted I was. However, with Debbie I felt I could get some biblical perspective on how I should go about conquering this through faith and religion. At 4 p.m., I headed to the NICU and went straight into the breast-pump room, then to see Noah. His occupational therapist (OT) had come to work on stretches with him, since Noah seemed not to be moving around and always had his hand in a fist. I asked her if this was due to his condition, and she said she didn't know but would give me exercises to work on with him so he could get comfortable with opening his hands and moving around. After watching the OT, I noticed Noah became so fatigued and drifted off to sleep, so I sat back in the chair and started to read my daily verse and daily devotional to him. I stayed there in the chair for what seemed like hours, just watching him, seeing him dream. When he would cry out, I would get up and sing, "Mommy's here, Noah's okay," and he would drift back to sleep and go back to dreaming. My mind started drifting. If only we could be in his nursery, dancing to music while I swayed him to sleep. If only I could lay him in his crib and put on his night stars for him. If only he could see his room and feel the warmth and love of all his family present in the room. My eyes began to water, and I had to continue to remind myself to stop, since they say babies can feel your energy, including anxiousness and sadness. When I knew I couldn't hold back the tears, because my chest hurt so badly, I told the nurse I would return later and left, noticing it was 7 p.m. By then my fiancé had picked me up, and we went to go eat to try to normalize the situation and come to terms with what was happening to us. We went to go have my favorite pizza at Raffalo's and discuss the pamphlets that were given to me by the doctor. I never had the courage to look at the DVD or even open the book to read it; I was scared and didn't want to believe this was real. However, I knew I had to read it and prepare myself for what was to come after Noah's surgeries. As I opened the folder, I realized what it was, and how the trach tube looked, and the Velcro neck ties that would wrap around his neck to hold the trach in place. I read the hospital plan that detailed the training we would receive before discharge, as well as CPR, stroller, and vent training. As I mentally prepared for what lay ahead, I just began to pray and kept repeating over and over that the Lord would not give me more than I could handle. I looked for support groups online and found one named Trach Mommies. I was able to finally read about other moms who were going through or had been through exactly what I was going through. I finally realized I wasn't alone in this, and if other women had gone through this and were in even worse positions, then I could overcome this with Jesus Christ, my Savior. As we went back to the Ronald McDonald House, I was emotionally drained from reading about what was to come. I would be lying to say I wasn't scared; however, I looked back at my life and saw the obstacles I had overcome and realized I was stronger than what I gave myself credit for. My son was half of me, and if he was already fighting for his life, then that was more than enough courage for me to be strong and do whatever I could to make sure my son was okay and to bring him home. Once back at the Ronald McDonald House, I began to pump and asked my fiancé if he could go by himself to tell Noah good night and send me a picture of him so I could see him. That night I finally had the strength to watch a sermon through my social media app, and I felt God was speaking to me through the message, which discussed Paul's famous message about overcoming hard times, and how hard times build endurance and character. I knew this was true, especially since my hard times had prepared me for this day. That night I closed my eyes, feeling I could take on whatever was thrown at me. I thanked God for this. Any moment of feeling okay or even a bit of peace was enough for me to smile and feel alive again.

October 18, 2019

That night I couldn't sleep. I knew in just a few hours my son would be undergoing surgery, and I was going to have to see Noah in pain. At 5 a.m., I pulled myself out of bed and went downstairs and made me a coffee. I felt so drained, my mind wouldn't let me relax. I felt it was going a mile a minute thinking about all the "what ifs." I had to gather myself and remember the verse that said to live in today. I went back upstairs, showered, and prayed for everything to go okay with my son, for him to wake up out of surgery, and of course to be shielded from pain. I got ready and headed to the hospital to meet my family. On arrival my mom, aunt, uncle, and cousin were there. They walked my fiancé and me to the NICU and told us they would wait in the waiting area for us. My fiancé and I walked in and went straight to see Noah. He was asleep and already had an IV in both his hand and his foot just in case one blew out. I whispered how much I loved him, and that he was going to be okay, and God was going to be with him. We held our hands and began to pray over Noah, asking for everything to go okay and of course for Noah to overcome this. The nurse walked in and told us that one parent could walk with the team downstairs to the OR. I looked at my fiancé and told him to go, that I wouldn't be able to walk away from him knowing what he was about to go through. I walked out of the NICU to meet my family, eyes watery, and they just hugged me and told me it was going to be okay; Noah was strong, and God was with us. We walked downstairs to the recovery waiting room, where I checked in and informed them that we would be waiting in the waiting area just in case a doctor needed to speak to us. The receptionist at the desk called the surgeon, and the surgeon came out and informed us that it shouldn't take longer than two hours, and we could look at the screen in the waiting room that showed when the surgery was over and when Noah would enter the recovery room. They told us once he was in the recovery room, he would be there for two hours, then placed back in the NICU, where we would be able to go up to see him. The surgeon looked at me and placed her hand on my shoulder and told me he was in good hands, and to go eat and get breakfast. I asked my family if we could go eat once we saw on the screen that Noah was in the surgery room, to which they all agreed. As I sat in the waiting room staring at the screen, I felt numb, as if I was physically there but my mind, body, and spirit were elsewhere. My eyes kept watering every time I thought about Noah in the recovery room by himself. I kept holding my breath, fighting back the tears, so I began to focus on different people in the waiting room who were doing exactly as I was doing, waiting for their loved one to make it out of surgery. I noticed a whole family there talking, keeping busy, and holding hands with one another like a unity chain for strength and support. I asked my uncle if we could all hold hands and pray; we gathered in a circle, held hands, and began to say a prayer for Noah. Once we saw he was in the operating room, which was at 10:30 a.m., we went to get breakfast in the cafeteria. I tried to muster up an appetite because I knew I needed fuel to stay awake and be there for Noah when he was back in the NICU. We all sat down and began talking. My family began to talk about things going on in their households as well as daily life activities. I knew they were trying to do this to get our minds elsewhere and focused on other things. We talked and talked for what felt like hours about biblical stories, worship songs, and how we needed to get together for the holidays so Noah could have his first holiday with his family. I didn't know how to break the news to them to inform them we were still going to be here for Thanksgiving, but I figured I would tell them as the date became closer. Around 12:30 p.m., I began holding my phone in my hand, waiting for the phone call from the doctor to tell me how the surgery went. As I sat there, an hour went by, then another, and my mind began racing, thinking the worst. They had told me it would only be a two-hour procedure, and we were now four hours, still waiting for news. My fiancé went down to the OR waiting room to look at the screen to see if maybe they had already placed him in the recovery room and tried to call for us in the waiting room. Once he returned, he informed me that the screen still said Noah was in the operating room. My heart sank, and I began to panic what was going on, what was happening. I began praying for Noah, hoping he was okay and there were no complications with his surgery. My family began to reassure me that he was okay, even though I could see the fear and concern in their eyes. We were sitting in the cafeteria when at 3:15 p.m. I received a phone call, and it was the surgeon. I ran to a quiet area and answered the phone.

"Is this the mother of Noah Peverell?"

"Yes, this is she."

"Hi. I just wanted to inform you everything went well. Sorry it took a little longer than usual. They were having issues placing his trach because of his short neck and had to wait for me to come out of surgery to go in and finish, but everything went well. He is in the recovery room, and he should be back in the NICU around 6 p.m."

My eyes immediately became watery, and I praised Jesus over and over, thanking Him for being with my son when I couldn't and making sure everything went okay. I walked back and told my family the great news, and we all rejoiced and hugged one another and thanked God for watching over Noah. We were finally able to breathe, and I finally felt the rock off my shoulders. My son was alive and well, and now we could start our journey to recovery and possibly heading home. We decided to go eat because my appetite had finally come back, since I no longer was worried about whether or not Noah was alive. We went to Los Burritos and just talked about what was to come and whether or not we thought we would be home for Halloween. I informed my family of the news that there was a high possibility we would be in the hospital until after Christmas, of course depending on Noah's recovery and how we were able to complete the training. I saw the disbelief in their faces, but my aunt and uncle had always had encouraging words for me and said, "I'm sure God will make sure you go home in the right timing, and of course when Noah is good and well to go home." I sat there and ate, thinking about all the things we had planned for Noah for Halloween and Thanksgiving, but I had to constantly bring my thoughts back to positivity and rejoice in what had happened today. My son was okay; he could now breathe on the ventilator, and no more fighting for his life to get air into his lungs. As 6 p.m. approached, we said good-bye to our family and entered the NICU to see Noah. When we approached pod G and no babies were in there, my heart sank, and I immediately went to the front and asked where Noah Peverell was located. The front-desk clerk informed me that they had moved Noah to pod A. I went over there, but before I entered, I had my fiancé go in to see if Noah was okay, since I was so afraid to see him hurt and in pain. Two minutes later he came outside and told me Noah was asleep, and it looked worse than what it was. I slowly walked in, my hands shaking and sweating. I arrived at Noah's bed and saw him lying there with stitches on his neck, a trach tube coming out of his neck, stitches around his belly button, and a G-tube placed on the side of his stomach. This was the first time I saw Noah with no tape and oxygen line on his face, and it was like seeing a brand-new Noah. His cheeks were red from the irritation of the tape, but his cheeks were full and plump. I saw the dried blood around his neck and asked the nurse if I could wipe him down, since he smelled of dried blood. The nurse told me I could as soon as he was up; they didn't want to wake him, since he had been given morphine for the pain and would probably be asleep for quite a while. I held his hand, stroking my thumb back and forth on top of his hand, singing in a whispered tone, "You are my sunshine, my only sunshine." I just watched and watched him, holding his hand, amazed, looking at the monitor that his oxygen levels were not desaturating, that his heart rate was stable, and no monitors were going off.

Around 7 p.m., the NICU closed, so we got our stuff and I kissed Noah and told him I would be back again once they opened around 8:30 p.m. Once we left the NICU, we saw my brother and his partner waiting there for us. They offered to take us to go eat dinner and to see how we were truly doing. I smiled as big as I could and told them I was okay. It was hard to see Noah all bandaged up, with stitches and dried blood around his body. It was also hard to see him swollen and lifeless, just imagining the pain he would wake up in. I wanted to be there once he awoke, but I knew I had to eat. My brother took me to one of my favorite pizza places that was right down the street from the hospital. Every part of my body begged to have a drink to release tension and stress; however, I needed to do everything in my power to try to produce more milk for Noah, especially since he would really need it now. I knew I had to rely on God to heal my pain and stress. I knew He must be the source I turned to, but my negative thoughts kept consuming me of how bad Noah's pain was. My fiancé tried to distract me and make me smile and handed me five dollars to play arcade games and win prizes to give to Noah one day. I tried my best to act happy and play a race car game; however, I didn't feel happy. I felt the way I always felt: how could I be happy and enjoy myself when my son was recovering and lying in dried blood? As soon as we were done eating and playing, I graciously thanked them for trying to keep my mind busy and preoccupied but said I needed to head back to the hospital to see if Noah had woken or not. I arrived right on time at 8:30 p.m. when the NICU opened. When I entered, I saw Noah squirming in his crib. The nurse told me his heart rate was high because of the pain he was in. Once I started to speak, I saw Noah slightly open his eyes. Once he did, he began to cry, but it was a silent cry; he had his mouth open and eyes closed shut as he was crying, but you could hear nothing. Before the trach, I was able to hear him cry out, and now it was complete silence. The only way I was able to know whether or not he was crying was if I was staring at his face. I tried my best to console Noah and gently rubbed my fingertips up and down his arm and told him his mom and dad were here and he would be okay. Shortly after that, the night doctor stepped in and talked about how Noah was doing much better since the placement of the trach and had no desaturations. I asked the doctor why I couldn't hear my son. I knew in the meeting they had explained that no air would pass through the voice box, which would leave Noah silent, but in all the commotion of everything, I hadn't stopped to think about what that meant. The doctor explained to me again why we could no longer hear him but said that down the line we might be able to hear little sounds. My heart hurt at that moment, and I came to the realization that in order for my son to breathe, he had to lose his voice. I shoved all my thoughts away and began to pray over Noah. I smiled at him and put on his lullabies and sang to him "Baby of Mine" until he went back to sleep. I informed the nurse to give Noah pain medicine around the clock, since I didn't want him in any more discomfort than what he needed to be.

At 10 p.m., we left the hospital and went back to our room. I couldn't get the thought out of my head that I wouldn't be able to hear my son. I was mad at myself for taking the little things for granted, like him crying. Now I would give anything to hear him again. I looked through my videos to see if at any point I had recorded Noah crying, and I was in luck. I had a ten-second video that his father had recorded when he was only one day old and entering the NICU. I replayed the video over and over and just sank to my feet and cried and cried. This would be the only memory I had of my Noah's voice, and I told myself I would listen to it every chance I got, no matter what painful memory it brought, no matter if it made me miss and realize I wouldn't hear my Noah for a long while. It was then that I began to contemplate and think about mothers who didn't care for their kids, how they were so selfish and ungrateful. Here I was, begging to hear my son, begging for him to be out of the hospital and in his home surrounded by love and family, when there were moms who abused their kids and could care less where their children ended up. It was then that I started drifting back to the unfairness of it all, going back to my negative views and thinking how unfair life was. My son was the only child in the NICU who had underwent a trach and a G-tube surgery. How was this fair? I was living a nightmare, not a fairy tale, how it should have been once a child was born. I had friends complaining about their children not listening and throwing tantrums, and the only thing I could ask them was whether or not their children could cry out, if they could hear their voices. Then I would tell them how lucky they were, what I would give for Noah to scream and cry again. They would apologize and say how ungrateful they were for not appreciating the little things in life. I would tell them how sorry I was for being so gloomy, but that I looked at life differently; it was the little things I was now realizing that counted, not the big things. The next day, in the morning we gave him a sponge bath and wiped away any remaining blood that was on his body. Dr. N. the ENT doctor who did the surgery, came over to check how the trach was healing. She removed the gauze and ties and replaced them. She informed me it was looking good and that in a couple of days she would be adding a new trach and removing stitches. When it was feeding time, I saw the nurses set up the Kangaroo pump with my breast milk and prepare the G-tube extension for my son's feeding. I saw the nurse open the Mic-Key button and place the G-tube extension. Once they popped the extension in, I saw my son wince and begin to move around once the extension was placed. The feeding began, and for the first time, I saw my son start to feed through his stomach with the feeding tube. It looked so easy to set up, but I was so afraid that every time the extension was inserted into the G-tube, my son would be in pain. However, I tried to keep my mind positive and remain happy that now my son no longer had a feeding tube down his nose. I saw a respiratory therapist come by his crib, and he introduced himself. He gave me the rundown of what he was doing and began to check Noah's chest with a stethoscope and placed his two fingers on his chest. Then he got a long plastic tube and connected it to the suction by the bed and opened sterile gloves and began to suction Noah's trach for any secretions. When I first saw this, my eyes began to water. I felt so emotional seeing this, especially knowing this would be the new norm for my son. Noah had so much discomfort on his face; all I could do was hold his hand and tell him he was going to be okay. The respiratory therapist began to tell me that at the hospital, they did a sterile-glove technique in order to make sure the catheter was clean when suctioning Noah. He showed me the numbers on the catheter and told me Dr. N. had informed them that they were using an 8 FR, which was the size of the catheter. They would stick the catheter down his trach to the number 8 (on the catheter) and suction him. He told me he would only tell me some information, since he didn't want me to feel overwhelmed by everything. He just looked at me, noticing me silently crying, and said, "It's going to be okay, Mom. Just remember that everything you will be doing is an act of love, and no matter the discomfort, Noah will know he is cared for." I began to cry harder and told myself repeatedly that I could do this, and Noah was just healing from a major surgery, so once recovered he would be fine. The respiratory therapist also cleared the condensation that built up in the ventilator tubes, so that no water would go down Noah's trach. I learned quickly that the condensation in Noah's vent circuit played a major role in how often he turned purple, as well as how to place the vent correctly so there was no weight pulling on the trach. After going outside to walk in the garden to take a mental break, I felt overwhelmed with everything I had seen and learned in those thirty minutes. This was Noah's and my life now; this was my new norm on top of having a new baby. Could I really do this? Was Noah just as afraid as I was? I began to think over and over of how badly I didn't want to fail my son.

I walked to get a coffee and calm my nerves and prayed. I noticed my anxiety and postpartum depression were all over the place. I couldn't keep my emotions in check; I would feel moments of hopelessness and couldn't fight it. I knew the time to fight it on my own was over. I needed support, therapy, and possibly even anxiety pills, but before I committed to anything, I wanted to make sure my son was okay and home. I walked back up to the NICU, more composed and confident in myself, even if I had to pretend. I walked in and saw Noah still lying in bed, repositioned and slightly moving. I walked over and began to rub my fingers through his head to play with his hair and comfort him as best as I could. As I stood next to him, the nurse stepped in to do a diaper change. Noah began to reposition himself, which caused the vent circuit to move to the right, which led to condensation going down his trach. Immediately I saw Noah clamp up and bear down and begin to turn purple. The monitor began to go off, and his oxygen level gradually began to decrease to 90, then shot down to 72. His heart rate started to decrease as well from 150 to 120. The nurse stepped in and immediately began to bag him while a respiratory therapist ran over to begin to suction his trach. Noah's color began to come back, and his vitals began to increase. I stood there, shocked like a deer in the headlights. I didn't understand why the purple desaturation episodes had begun to occur again. As often as I had seen Noah turn purple and desaturate, it was a sight I couldn't get used to. As much as my body said for me to run toward him to help, I just stood there frozen, not moving, screaming on the inside for Noah to breathe. Once he was stable, I saw he had another poop in his diaper, and he went into a deep sleep as though he was overwhelmed and tired from the episode that had occurred. I looked at the nurse and respiratory therapist and asked why he was still turning purple. Was this something that was going to continue? I had thought the trach would stop all this from occurring. The nurse began to explain to me that it could occur if Noah clamped down as he did, which caused the air coming out of the vent not to reach his lungs accordingly. On top of that, holding his breath could cause the desaturation episodes. I kind of understood at the time, but what scared me the most was the fact that I had thought our purple days were over. Shortly after the MD came over and asked what had happened and how low Noah's vitals went, he began to explain as well that Noah tended to clamp down and hold his breath when he was in distress, which could force the air not to go into his lungs. I asked the doctor how to prevent the clamping and holding the breath, stressing to him there ought to be something we could do to help him. The doctor looked at me with a smile and told me it would take time. With the help of the OT and me, Noah would begin to see that he was okay and know positive touch, which could cause him not to be distressed. The nurse also stepped in and said that right now, touch to Noah was negative because of the surgeries as well as other things, such as the pain he had experienced. As much as I already knew he was traumatized, I didn't want to admit it. I had promised myself that my son would not live a rough childhood as I did, not have trauma or side effects, just a happy childhood with a boy knowing his two parents loved him tremendously. However, that wasn't the case. Anytime Noah was touched by medical gloves, he became upset and cried, sometimes so upset it led to a desaturation. He became so traumatized with a simple diaper change that as soon as he felt a medical glove touch his skin, he would cry and begin kicking, bucking, and trying to scream. As a mother, it killed me inside to see Noah suffer from trauma, and it broke me to know that already, at a very young age, Noah was experiencing this. Who knew a simple touch to his skin would freak him out and make him cry? And it all began after surgery. I left for home early that night. I felt defeated, as though I couldn't win no matter how hard I tried. I felt that as a mother, I was failing. I couldn't help or protect my son no matter what I did, and on top of everything else, even a simple touch made him scared to the point of shaking. I wanted to tell him so badly and make him understand that this wasn't life. It wasn't constant pain and loneliness; there was love, laughter, and fun. I called for a shuttle and cried all the way back home. I knew the driver could hear my sobs, and I'm sure he had an idea of my pain, but he just kept driving and pretended as if he didn't hear anything. As soon as I was dropped off at the Ronald McDonald House, I rushed to the room and lay down and continued to cry for thirty minutes straight, just holding on to my chest, feeling as if my heart was about to break.

The next day, I awoke determined to think positive and see it as a new day worth fighting for. I went downstairs to get the breakfast they were serving. I ate, then pumped and made my way to the hospital. As I entered, I said hi to the familiar faces, then went up to the NICU. Upon my entering, the respiratory therapist and nurse were there and greeted me. I asked how Noah's night was, and they told me he had been a little fussy due to the pain, but they had started to give him Tylenol as needed. I told the nurse again to give it to him every four hours; I didn't want him to feel any discomfort, especially since he was moved from position to position every three hours. The respiratory therapist asked me how I was feeling; today was the day they were going to have me suction him multiple times. I felt so nervous and scared. Seeing the trach in my son still terrified me, but I told myself, *I must do this. The more I do it, the more familiar it will become.* The nurse looked at me and said, "You can do it." I smiled and began to take off my sweater; that's how much I was nervously sweating. Finally, I put on the gloves and picked up the catheter, placed my finger on the number eight on the catheter, and removed the ventilator and began to suction my son's trach. I did it for three seconds, as instructed, and reconnected my son's ventilator. I noticed for the first time that when the ventilator was off my son, his oxygen level began to drop. I didn't understand, since he was awake. The respiratory therapist gave me feedback on how to use one hand to remove the circuit on the ventilator and the other hand to suction. It made sense, since I felt I was all over the place and taking a long time to suction. The respiratory therapist told me that in the next two hours, he would be changing the trach ties and gauze with the nurse, and asked whether or not I would be here so I could witness it. I told them yes, I would, and expressed I wanted to learn as much as possible. I kissed my son's hand and told him Mommy was here; then I began to sing his lullabies to him. I began to play with his hair and read him the books I had for him. He had a wide smile every time he heard my voice. I began to talk to him about how much I missed him when he was away, and how I couldn't wait to be home in his room with his dogs and family. I told him about his crib, how he had his own room, and Grandma was coming that day to see him. An hour later, I was able to witness the respiratory therapist and nurse complete the trach care, and it absolutely broke my heart. I saw the nurse swaddle him so his arms wouldn't escape, and use another hospital blanket to secure the swaddle, since Noah tended to break free and kick and fight when they were doing the trach care. The respiratory therapist began to hold the trach and explained to me that two people should always do this: one person as the captain, who would pretty much take control and tell the second person what steps to take. The nurse began to untie the ties and clean around Noah's neck with Q-tips and gauze dipped in a fifty-fifty solution of water and peroxide. Once his neck was clean, they removed the front Mepilex dressing, which was around the front of the trach, and began to clean around the stoma hole with Q-tips. A brand-new Mepliex dressing was placed around the trach site, and the Velcro ties were wrapped around his neck and tightened so the trach could be held into place. However, while all this was occurring, Noah was fighting. He was kicking, pushing his arms out, crying, desaturating, turning purple, and becoming rigid. A fifteen-minute procedure took almost forty-five minutes because of the battle with him. I could see the pain he felt when he was being moved, especially his neck. I saw the screams and kicks once he felt the medical gloves touch his skin. All I could do was stand there and watch, and no matter how badly I wanted to say, "Stop, he is in pain," I knew the trach care had to be done to make sure the area was clean. This was now his new daily-life procedure that would need to be done. As a mother, seeing my child in pain and not being able to do anything but try to calm him and hold him down so they could complete the procedure was devastating. I felt as if I was betraying him, as if he knew it was me, his mom, holding him down while he was fighting in pain and I did not stop it. From the struggle of him moving his neck and trying to fight the hands off him, I saw the trach pop out and be placed back in, and Noah obtained a cut on his neck from the Velcro ties. After the trach care, they saw the terror in my face and told me to go eat and come back, and they could go over other things like his G-tube. *Lord, I know You do not give more than someone can bear, but Father, when will this madness end? When will Noah get better? When will we get to the point of normalcy? How can I be strong and brave even though I want to scream out because my son is in pain?*

That night I did not return until after eight. I was scared about what I had witnessed, and to know that was going to be my son's daily life twice a day shocked me. This was my new normal, and I had to become adjusted to it fast. When I came back, I kissed Noah, who was still there motionless with stitches still on his G-tube and stomach area. My eyes began to water, and I began to apologize to him for not being strong, for not staying, and for it being overwhelming for me. That day I brought my Bible and read a page to him. While he slept, I was able to find worship lullabies, where it had songs such as "Make Me Brave" by Bethel, and that is when I began to sing it to him each time he was asleep, as well as "Our God" by Chris Tomlinson. I would always hum "Make Me Brave" to Noah, and after a couple of days, it was as if he knew the song and smiled every time I sang it to him. He was the most important thing in my life. This little baby was my entire world, and he gave me the motivation to continue to fight, especially because he woke up every day fighting to be here. God did the rest—He gave me the armor of God. Every night before shift change, the maintenance worker cleaned the pod and mopped the floors around the pod. She always heard me singing and humming to Noah and turned to me and smiled. One day she asked me what I was singing, and I told her "Make Me Brave." She smiled and said, "You are a great mom." Even though she did not know me or anything about my situation and what I was going through, that comment meant so much to me. Again, sometimes we do not see the smallest things God does for us, or the people He places in our lives. A simple comment from her made my day, and I was able to walk out of the NICU with my head held high, feeling I could be a great mom to Noah no matter what came our way.

October 31, 2019

    Halloween had arrived and we were still in the hospital. Every day we were learning little by little how to tend to Noah, including how to clean his G-tube area and set up his feeding pump to feed him. We learned how to flush out the bag with water after feeding him and how to insert his G-tube extension. For a couple of days, I was so scared to insert the extension to his G-tube. Even though they told me over and over that he would feel little discomfort, I was still so afraid. It felt as if I was pushing down so hard against his stomach just to hear the little click. If I could not do it the first time, I would call the nurse over to do it. Luckily, Noah had a great nurse, Daphnee, who was patient with me and told me that Noah ate every three hours, so I would be trying each time he ate as long as she was on shift. She was a good nurse; she taught me a lot about the G-tube and always paid close attention to Noah. She never panicked when he turned purple, just tried to stimulate him by hitting his back and talking to him so he could relax and release his clamp down. The night before, a nurse had informed me that she would be stopping by the pod to take a picture of the NICU babies in their Halloween costume for their first Halloween. I was overjoyed because I had thought the Dumbo costume I purchased would go to waste. Noah's dad and I were able to buy elephant T-shirts to match Noah's costume to at least be in the Halloween spirit, and so Noah could look back and have memories and know we did everything we could to make it enjoyable for him. The next day, for Halloween I went early, dressed in my costume, ready to celebrate Halloween the best way I knew how, full of joy and of course spending time with Noah. I dressed him up in his Dumbo costume, which was the cutest thing ever. His doctor and nurse were able to come by to see his costume, which they thought was so adorable. I brought in the Halloween books I had previously purchased, so I could read to him. Soon after, a nurse came in and did a whole photo shoot for Noah. She decorated his crib to have a Halloween background and started snapping pictures. It was then I realized my Noah was a social butterfly, a natural charmer. He loved the attention he was receiving to smile, the clapping and laughter we displayed due to how cute he was. For that moment, seeing that part of him, knowing he was smiling and having an enjoyable time despite the situation we were in and the pain of the trach, put a fire under me to see that my son was strong, God was here, and he was going to be okay. The nurse printed out the picture and put it in a Halloween frame and handed it to us. I smiled so much and wanted to hug the nurse. No matter how small the gesture was, it meant the world to me, especially since I was feeling down about celebrating Halloween in the hospital. It was little things like that I will never forget, and she will never know that the kind gesture meant the world to me. I can never thank her for that, besides hold her in a special place in my heart and memory.

That night we went back to the Ronald McDonald House, ate dinner, and played dominoes. I think we both took that night as a win because we were trying to attempt to spend time together no matter our current circumstance. The next week was filled with uncertainty, even though Noah was thriving, and we were at a point of Noah just needing to gain weight so we could try him on the home ventilator. During this time, my fiancé and I began to take a turn for the worse. We began arguing every day, taking our frustrations out on each other. It came to a point where we could not be around each other. We produced a schedule where we would visit Noah at separate times. Everyone had started to warn me about this occurring, especially my family. They would always tell me that we needed to build our relationship as strong as ever because if not, we would begin to take our stress and anger out on each other. Unfortunately, that's what occurred. I felt so alone and broken. At a time when we both needed each other the most, we were acting like enemies. I would wake up in dismay; I could no longer visit my son at night because my fiancé was there. To avoid any arguments, I would not go. I would go home and try to sleep. I had no place of refuge. I could no longer go back to the room to cry because now I was in a room with someone I was at odds with and could not tell how I felt because of the strain, hurt, and anger. There were nights when I would lie on the opposite bed and cry myself to sleep. We no longer shared a bed, just a room, where we acted like the other person did not exist. I would wake up early, shower, get ready, and go be with Noah until 4 p.m. We had to meet when Noah's dad was off work in order to do our trach-care training together. You can only imagine the tension in the room with us trying to work together as a team. We would become loud with each other, not work as a team, even to the point where the nurse would intervene and ask us to debrief to go over how we could work together. My fiancé and I would talk about it, see where we went wrong, and try to produce solutions. However, each day at 4 p.m. was the worst time of day for me. I hated that he wanted to be in control and always took charge of changing Noah's trach care. He never trusted me to care for Noah or gave me the benefit of the doubt. Soon belittlements began of him calling me stupid, telling me I did not know what I was doing, to every horrible thing you can imagine. I remember one night after Noah's trach care, we began arguing back and forth as we were walking out of the hospital because he was telling me that I didn't help him and made him do everything without being a team player. I was so upset and told him I couldn't work with him when he was getting loud and causing scenes with nurses and other parents present. He began to tell me that it was not his fault and I was a stupid ass, and I walked away. I walked home in the rain that day because I didn't want to be around him. I did not understand how he could be so mean to me during a time when I was utterly broken. I was going through the wringer, and I had only him. He was my family now—he and Noah—yet he was treating me like I was absolutely nothing to him. During this time, we were coping with what was occurring in our own way and methods. He was staying out late drinking and smoking, while I would go to the room and cry and cry. It felt as though my whole world was falling apart and I had no one to rely on. My partner was out, while I was alone. All I wanted was for him to continue to hold me, tell me it was going to be okay, that we were going to make it, but soon after, he became annoyed with me. He couldn't understand why I couldn't be strong, why I couldn't stop crying and fight through this. It felt as if he began to despise me, and he told me that I was not a strong woman, and what a woman should be. I was devastated. This was my fiancé telling me these things. Everything was over. I didn't know how to continue, and I just began praying. I prayed for me to beat the depression, for Noah's health, and for our relationship to make it. This was not who we were—it is what we had become—and I didn't know what the outcome might be, but I seemed to know where we were headed. That night my fiancé stayed out late; he had asked me if it would be okay if he stayed out to clear his mind. I told him it was fine, and that I would be going to sleep early. That night I woke up at 2 a.m. and noticed he was not home. I had no text messages or missed calls explaining where he was. I called him and asked him where he was, and he told me he was on Alvarado Street, which was a rough area in Los Angeles known for drugs and prostitution. I began to think the worst and asked him why he was there, and began to tell him what that area was known for, and how could he be there when I needed him home with me, comforting me, especially knowing I couldn't go through this alone? At this time, I was so broken that I wrote him a letter that night telling him I couldn't do this anymore. I couldn't be depressed, be the best for Noah, and try to fix this relationship. I told him I needed a partner to uplift me, not belittle me, and to be there for me. I expressed this was not an engagement. He didn't seem like a man who loved me, and he was being selfish at this point. I expressed I wanted to call off the engagement until we could fix this, and I placed the ring on that letter. The next day, I headed early to the hospital. I was so hurt and just wanted to be with Noah and feel peace, happiness, and comfort. When I got there, the nurse told me the next step would be to get Noah to PICU, which meant we were one step closer to going home. We needed to do a few more trainings, and Noah needed to gain weight. He was seven pounds five ounces; one more pound and then we would be able to go upstairs and start our journey home. I asked if he had gained any more weight, since they obtained an official weight at the beginning of each morning shift. The nurse told me no but to be hopeful since it was only one pound, and it could take a matter of days or weeks, of course, depending on Noah. I sang with Noah and read him the devotional that day. I needed all the strength I could get. He seemed so happy. He kept smiling and held on to my finger as I sang my papisito to him. Around this time, I received a call from my sister-in-law, asking me what had happened and whether or not I was okay. I stepped out of the room and explained to her what had happened between her brother and me, that I needed a break from trying to make this work and didn't want to be engaged while all this was occurring, and we couldn't seem to get along. I confided in her and told her how broken I was, how his words had cut me, and I had no more strength in me and needed all the strength I had left for Noah. I couldn't break down; Noah needed to know his mom was right by his side no matter the circum-stance. Just then I received a message from Noah's dad stating he was 110 percent done with me and did not want to be near or around me, so to let him know when I left the hospital so he could see Noah. I was so upset by his response and told him I would be there until 4 p.m. After Noah's trach care, I would leave so he could visit Noah. My heart was broken, but I wiped off the tears, put on the happiest face I could, and walked back into the NICU, pretending as if my world was not falling apart. I am always amazed how in difficult situations the Lord will do things and intervene to show, no matter how dark the tunnel is, He is there right by your side. Just then the nurse who had taken the Halloween photos walked in and asked me how I was. I told her I was the best I could be. She then informed me that she had spoken with the PICU and asked if she could get a PICU crib for Noah, since he was outgrowing the pod and needed an actual crib. I was so happy just then my face lit up, and she told me she was on her way up to the fourth floor to get it. I then began to clean out Noah's pod and collect anything in it to transition it to his new crib. Shortly after, the nurse arrived with the crib, and I was so overloaded with happiness. In came a big white crib with rails and a full mattress that was at an incline and had a pillow where Noah could peacefully sleep without being smushed with wires and tubes everywhere. I was able to decorate his crib with Noah's dad's teddy bear he had given him, "Pumpkin Bear," in one corner of the crib and his devotional books in another. The nurse walked in again with a mobile and asked me if I wanted it for Noah. I said yes and thanked her over and over for her kindness and told her how much it meant to me. We set up the mobile, and I held Noah as the respiratory therapist and nurse began to set up all the wiring for him. As soon as all the wires were placed, Noah was put in his crib and the mobile began to spin and play music. Immediately Noah began to smile and stare at the mobile, since he was seeing one for the first time. That smile on his face was everything I needed in that moment. Everything negative in my life seemed to disappear, and it was just Noah and I enjoying something so normal as a crib and a mobile playing music. Again I thanked the nurse over and over. This nurse who seemed to keep helping Noah and me was not his assigned nurse; she was a nurse that would walk around and check in, and for some reason, she always kept an eye on Noah and checked in with me. Why she did this I will never know, but I know it was someone God sent to me to help in my time of need. I know He did it so I wouldn't feel alone, especially when I was in desperate need of something good going my way and had someone to be there for me. Time passed; it was 4 p.m.

and Noah's dad walked in. I could feel the tension rolling off him, the anger he had toward me, and I knew it was not healthy to have this around Noah, especially since he was here in the hospital fighting to make it out. I told the respiratory therapist that I had to do an errand, so if he could, please fill in for me and help Noah's dad with the trach care. He agreed and told me he would go over the trach change, since Noah's dad needed to do one more so we could finish the training in the NICU. I told Noah's dad I would be stepping out and gave Noah the biggest kiss and walked out of the NICU, half crying because I didn't want to leave my son and half crying because I was starting to lose the family that I had always wanted and imagined would be.

November 2, 2019

The next couple of days, everything was still the same. Noah's dad and I were not talking. We did not speak a word to each other and made sure to have a different schedule on when we visited Noah. Noah's dad went back to work while we still stayed in the Ronald McDonald House. By the time I woke up to pump and get ready to see Noah, he was gone. When he was out from work and ready to see Noah, he would let me know he was on his way and I would get my stuff ready to leave. As I was on my way, I felt I couldn't take it anymore, being alone. I hadn't reached out to anyone or expressed anything I was going through. For whatever reason, I wanted everyone to believe I was doing okay and was making it through like a strong Christian woman would. However, I was so tired of carrying that image. I wasn't strong. Yes, I had faith and prayed, but I wasn't sure I was going to make it out. I was tired physically, emotionally, and mentally. I had nothing more to give. As my son was getting better, my relationship was falling apart, and I didn't know what this meant for us and our journey home, whether or not we were going to survive this. I was not talking to my best friend; at the time, we were at odds, and I didn't try reaching out to explain everything I was going through. I felt she wouldn't understand because she was living the single life and couldn't give me the advice I needed. I reached out to my mom, who had been there for me during this time but on her own terms. She would come only if she wasn't depressed or suffering from anxiety that day, or if she didn't have to be around Noah's dad, since they weren't getting along. I wanted to have my mom with me during this difficult time, but it was only if she felt up for it, which was hurtful at the time because I needed my mom. However, I still wanted her there no matter how little time she could offer. I texted her and told her Noah's dad and I weren't doing well and asked if she could come down to see me, since I was always alone and needed someone to be there for me. But she told me she couldn't, that she had the responsibility of taking and picking up my sixteen-year-old niece from high school. I just hung up the phone and didn't know what to say. I was hurt all over again. The one person I thought would be there for me had other priorities ahead of what I was going through. I didn't understand how I could tell her everything I was going through on top of her grandson being in the intensive care unit, it still wasn't enough for her to drop everything and come down to see me. From there on out, I knew I was alone, and I really couldn't depend on anyone but myself. I was back to being that twelve-year-old child who was let down by her mom all over again. I went back to the Ronald McDonald House and lay down and cried and cried. It was as if life was hitting me left and right and trying to knock out any little strength I had left in me. I begged and pleaded with God to please let me feel Him, to please hug me, rub my hair, and tell me everything was going to be okay, to be the father I never had. I begged, saying, "Please, Father, please, just hug me and give me that peace I once felt with You." After what seemed like hours of crying, I realized it was late and it was time to get up and go eat before Ryan came back and saw me an emotional mess. I didn't want him to know I felt as if I was dying inside because of everything that was happening. I felt he would never understand me, nor I him. I stood up and thought of all the places in LA that I hadn't been to in quite a while and remembered a pho place where I used to go with my family years ago when everything was normal. It was hard driving around town, even being around people, because even though it was early November, many places were already decorated for Christmas. It was a constant reminder that I was going through a challenging time stuck in a different town and in the hospital during the holidays. I didn't feel cheerful at all; I wanted to pretend as if nothing was going on and I was just happy and content in my life. I had gone through so much, and even though I tried to look at the positivity of everything, I felt as though I couldn't win, and the negative was outweighing the positive. As I entered the restaurant by myself, I noticed the whole restaurant decorated with Christmas lights, and I sat there able to see multiple families cheerful. I felt overwhelmed and thought that maybe if I showed Noah's dad kindness during this time, we could both wave the white flag and come together to work as a team for Noah's sake. So I gave in and decided to text him and let him know I was eating at a restaurant and asked if he wanted something to eat. He responded to not text him and to leave him alone. I felt a punch to my gut. Maybe I set myself up for failure, but I had thought maybe, just maybe, we could see the love we once had for each other and realize we needed each other right now. I wanted both of us to be present around Noah without the big elephant in the room. After that message, it was like another chip to my heart breaking off. I tried my best to eat, but I was no longer hungry. I paid my bill and went to my car as my eyes began to tear up, thinking what my life had come to. Never did I think I would be in this position. I had thought I was finally going to get my fairy tale, a happily ever after, Noah being a healthy baby boy. Just then "Jingle Bell Rock" came on the radio, and I just put my head down and cried. My reality was my son was in the hospital, my relationship was over, and my relationships with my mom, sister, and best friend were nonexistent. I went home, put a blanket over my head, and fell into a deep sleep.

November 8, 2019

By this time, I had formed a great relationship with Noah's OT, Diane. Noah seemed to love her soft, gentle singing voice. Every time she would come around, he would smile and get so happy. She expressed to me that at this time she had made splints for his hands, since he was now holding his hands as fists and bending his wrists to grab things. The main purpose of the splints was to enable him to properly open his hands and keep his wrists straight. She told me she had just informed the nurses that Noah had to have the splints on two hours, then off two hours. I asked her if we were going to go back to trying to feed Noah, since he was eating before the trach surgery. She informed me that they would try, and she would come the next day with a bottle to try to feed him again. She wanted to build him up to drinking ten milliliters so he could have a swallow test done again to check if he was now swallowing correctly. I was so excited. If he could eat, then maybe we wouldn't have to do all his feedings through the G-tube; that was my initial thought. She showed me exercises I could do with him and stretches for his whole body, since he was hardly moving in the bed. I was grateful for her; she taught me so much about range of motion for Noah, and oral exercises to get him used to swallowing. I knew the G-tube had been placed as a precaution, but I also wanted to see if Noah would be able to eat again on his own. After Diane left, I was able to go to the cafeteria and grab a coffee. The young cashier already knew me at this point; no matter if I ordered a small coffee, she always gave me a large. Again, I didn't know if I wore it all over my face, but she was one of those individuals I felt that God sent my way just to say "I am here." Even if it was just a bigger size of coffee that she gave me, at the time I needed it. It brought a smile to my face, knowing I was going to get a little more coffee that day, and for that I thanked God. I grabbed my coffee and went outside to get fresh air and try to replay and write down in my notes everything I had learned today so I could do these activities and exercises with Noah once I was home. It was weighing heavily on my heart to stop doing this alone and to reach out to others asking for help, even if it was just to speak to someone about what was going on. I don't know why, but I felt so shameful and guilty about what was happening to me. I wasn't raised to ask anyone for help, but I knew my anxiety and depression were so high that I needed an outlet, that I needed someone to vent to even if it was only to get someone to hear me. I reached out to the woman I looked up to and knew would hold no judgment against me regarding my wavering faith and faulty relationship. I emailed Debbie again; she immediately called me and said she was glad I reached out to her. She asked if she could stop by over the weekend so she could visit Noah and take me out to lunch to get away and just talk and be there for me. I told her that of course I would love to see her and asked if she could come in the morning, since I didn't want any conflict between Noah's dad and I over visiting times with Noah. I felt relieved after getting off the phone with her. I wished I had done it sooner. All this time, I had felt I couldn't reach out to anyone because no one would understand. Also, I didn't want to tell the truth about my deteriorating relationship, how four months ago my fiancé and I had been utterly in love with each other, on cloud nine waiting for Noah to be born, and talking about our fantasy life. We had imagined Noah getting older and us moving to Acton to build our dream home and farmland, and yet here we were in the hospital, trying to see Noah recover, not engaged anymore, hating each other and not even on speaking terms. I didn't know how to tell someone what was happening or where to even begin. How does something go from beautiful to ugly in a matter of four months? Who knows? But I was finally ready to reach out for help and tell someone what was really happening, and that I needed any help and prayers that I could get. It was around 3 p.m. by then, so I headed back upstairs to spend my final hour with Noah. When I arrived, Noah was up, staring at his mobile. I asked the nurse if I could hold him, and she said of course. Finally, I was able to hold my son whenever I wanted. I held on to him so tight; I was trying my hardest to get used to the circuit on the ventilator and making sure the trach was okay. It was something new for me, trying to get used to all the wiring and knowing this was going to be my new norm. I was always going to have to be careful with his trach, no matter if I was holding him, placing him in a car seat, placing him in a stroller, or even just moving anywhere with him. When 4 p.m. hit, Noah's dad walked in, and it was time for us to get ready to do the trach ties. I handed Noah over to him as I began to prepare and set up the trach supplies, since it was going to be my turn to lead when we did the care. During this time, Noah was swaddled twice with blankets, along with another blanket over his feet, since he would kick, scream, and try to break free during the trach care. As I angled the bed and told everyone I was ready, the nurse and respiratory therapist stepped in to watch us in order to give us advice and tell us what we could do better. As I started and began telling Noah's dad to turn Noah's neck so I could unhook the tie, he began to sigh and speak in a stern voice, which I knew at this moment that this was going to be one of those nights when he was not willing to work with me. As we continued and I was cleaning Noah's neck, Noah began crying, kicking, and moving around, trying to break loose out of the swaddle. At this moment, Noah's dad became upset and began blaming me for not putting the swaddle tight enough, and he was having trouble holding the trach in while Noah was fidgeting and crying. As soon as the respiratory therapist saw the frustration and tone level of Noah's dad's voice, he asked if he could step in so he could hold the trach while Noah's dad held Noah's legs. I began to try to hurry to finish because at this time Noah was kicking and screaming. When we were finally done, the respiratory therapist and nurse said we had done a good job, and we just needed to work on communication and being patient with each other. At this point, I was so upset and suppressing my anger, trying not to explode. I tried to work and talk to Noah's dad in a calm and collected manner but was always met with opposition. He would always raise his voice and sternly command things instead of speaking to me like a normal individual. What upset me the most was the fact that we were in a small space; each pod held five other babies, along with five other families and nurses, and here they were all witnessing this unfold. They heard the angry tone between us, and I felt, instead of him choosing to pretend to be okay, he was displaying this in front of everyone, including Noah, who was still recovering. I felt, How could he be this way with me? How could he treat me in this manner? I was still suffering from postpartum depression, my C-section, my sanity, and it still wasn't enough for him to call a truce. I didn't know how this man I once loved could treat me this way, how he couldn't see how desperately I needed help, in pain and suffering, and how he couldn't lay his anger aside and at least talk to me with respect or at least put on a show. I was always embarrassed to walk out of there; the nurses never knew what to say, and the families around would just stare, wondering what was going on. As I walked out feeling defeated, I tried to think about tomorrow and all the positive things that would be happening: Noah getting bottle-fed again and of course Debbie coming to see Noah and me. I went back to the Ronald McDonald House, since there was going to be a church stopping by to host dinner for us. Even though I didn't like to go because I felt this was rock-bottom living off charity, I tried to hold my head up high and remind myself to take the help when I needed it; and of course, after the rain, the sun does shine. As I lined up with other families waiting to be served food, I noticed all the other little children who were there with some form of disability, including cancer. No matter how many different families I saw, it amazed me how the parents walked around with such big smiles on their faces, comforting their children and being the beacon of light that their children needed. I never forgot one family; they touched my heart and really opened my eyes to see that I should not view Noah as just a disabled child, but as a child of hope, strength, love, and, most important, a child of God. One dad and his daughter were also in the kitchen-stove area, cooking food. I noticed they often came in late, since I was often down there around 8 p.m. (trying to avoid families just so I could be alone). I didn't know the little girl's condition, but she was disfigured. Even though she was, her father treated her absolutely normal. He would cook on the stove while she sat on the countertop, holding her radio to her ear and singing oldies aloud. It warmed my heart to see how this father treated her so normally, with such care and love. It was then that I realized it was up to me to treat Noah how I wanted him to be treated. I could either close him off to the world, scared of the stares and what others would think, or I could treat him normally, like any boy growing up in a loving family. It was one of those things where you never thought it would happen to you, or that you would be saying you had a special needs child, but I had to come to terms with the fact that I did. Even if I got stares or questions from people who knew no better, and no matter what came my way, I had to be prepared to accept those things and be strong enough to teach Noah that he was normal, just with special qualities. I didn't want to think about the bad anymore, even though it was hard not to wonder if Noah would be able to run one day or play baseball and basketball as we always wanted. I came back to reality and finished making a pizza and took a notebook with me so I could start writing down any questions I had for the doctor, and any information the nurses and doctors gave me. During this time, I had realized I was going through some form of shell shock. I didn't want to self-diagnose myself, but I noticed I no longer remembered anything. If someone told me something, I would immediately forget it unless I wrote it down, which was uncommon for me. So I tried to write as much as I could, such as anything I was going through, because I didn't want to forget, and I wanted to be sure I was well aware of Noah's condition and could do what I could to help him. As I jotted down some things that happened that day, everything I had learned from the OT, Diane, I noticed the time and realized how late it was. It was time for me to go to bed. I was excited to see Debbie tomorrow, just to have a friend. It was finally time to tell someone what I was going through; I just didn't know where to start.

Saturday, November 9, 2019

I woke up at 6 a.m. and decided to treat myself to breakfast. I went to McDonald's and ordered my favorite, a sausage McMuffin and a caramel frappe, and headed to the hospital. As soon as I walked in, I asked the nurse if Noah had gained any weight. He said he had gained two ounces, which meant we were just twelve ounces away from going upstairs to the PICU. I was happy to hear any good news. I asked how his night was, and they reported to me he had no episodes of desaturations, which was a good thing. I decided to do skin-to-skin. Noah was happy and began suckling; I was so happy because it was the first time he seemed interested to try to breastfeed. After thirty minutes of this, he fell asleep in my arms, and I began to play his favorite lullabies and sing to him. Once 10 a.m. hit, I knew Debbie would be on her way, so I put Noah back in his crib and made sure to be able to look out for her call, since it was a process to get inside the NICU. Once I went outside, I saw Debbie and greeted her with a hug. I was so relieved she was here. I don't know if it is wrong to say this, but I always felt she was the closest thing I had to Jesus; she was so genuinely nice and a great Christian woman. I always felt that with her around and speaking to her, I was getting the closest godly advice I could come to. It wasn't about what she did; it was about her presence. It was something you just wanted to be around, so much positivity and hope. As I brought her to the NICU, I introduced her to my son, who was lying there, eyes open, looking at his mobile. She smiled at him and talked to Noah. She couldn't believe how cute he looked and how much he resembled me. I told her how much I couldn't believe he came out looking exactly like me. Seeing side-by-side comparisons of me when I was younger, he looked like my twin. After thirty minutes of Debbie visiting with Noah, we headed to cafeteria for lunch. As we walked, she told me she had no idea what was going on and felt so bad not to have been there for me. I told her not to feel that way, that it was me shutting off the world on what was happening because I wanted to be alone, and the truth of the matter was, I felt as if I was in a dark hole and was scraping to get out. I explained what had happened during pregnancy, from the fluid in Noah's brain to other respiratory issues happening, which they didn't know why the brain was not sending signals to his lungs, to him having to breathe through a trach. As I sat there explaining, trying not to cry, she asked me how I was holding up. I wanted to just cry, but since we were in a cafeteria full of doctors and nurses, I held myself together and told her the truth. I told her I felt I was shutting down, that there were days of positivity and hope where I felt I could take on the world, and then there were days where I felt it was the end of the world and I had to muster all the strength I had to get ready and come to the hospital. I also told her the truth: I was fighting a spiritual battle every day within myself. Some days I had the biggest faith and was hopeful and felt happy, and on other days, I felt life was unfair and wondered why this was happening to me, let alone to Noah. I told her how I felt as a Christian. I was wrong for thinking that way, of life being so unfair and why me, but I was angry, not at God but at my situation. Why did it have to be this hard? Why did my child have to suffer, and why did I feel as if I was living every mother's worst nightmare instead of dancing around with my child in a fairy tale? I didn't know how to feel anymore, or which emotion or way of thinking was correct. Once she let me rant and express everything, her eyes were watery and she told me how sad she was to see me hurting, and that even though she would never understand what I was going through, I had every right to feel this way. She expressed it was okay to feel angry, as if it was unfair, or even to say, "Why did this happen to me?" She stated, "We are all human. We have feelings and thoughts, and Jesus knows this. It's what you do with it. If you pick yourself up, look at the blessings, and keep going, then you will feel better, rather than dwelling on things that can't be changed." She expressed for me to reach out to God to receive some clarity on why me. She told me to ask God to help me understand what was going on, the "why," and of course to make me see He was here. I told her that was the thing I knew, that He was here. He had showed me so many signs that He was here, from random people asking to pray for me, asking me about my story, extra giving toward me, and of course Noah always being placed in my favorite number and basketball number, three or thirty-three. That was why I felt so guilty about feeling this was unfair. I knew that despite my situation and all my sins throughout my life, when I needed Him, He was here. No matter what I had done, He was here. I always tried to view God as a person here. I felt that when you hurt Him over and over and expected Him to turn away from you, He was still there helping you; and you think about how selfish and messed up you have been for being hurtful to God, who has always been there. No matter how much I hurt Him, God had always shown me grace. I opened up to her and told her the deepest pain and suffering I was feeling: walking out each night without Noah. Every night, no matter what day or time, it killed me to have to leave without him, to let him stay in the hospital alone. It killed me walking out of the hospital each and every night without my child, hoping he didn't notice I was gone, hoping he wasn't calling out for me, and hoping he wasn't waiting for me to come. I prayed every night that he wouldn't feel alone, or that I had abandoned him. I wished I could explain why I had to leave him there, and make him understand. A night or two I could have dealt with, but here we were going on two months, and no matter how long it had been, each night it stabbed me in my heart. I didn't want anyone to feel sad for me or pity me, because everyone has their own struggles they are dealing with. But when I looked at Debbie, I knew she had no judgment in her eyes, and it made me feel better because at that time and place, I felt I was a failure as a mother. I couldn't protect my child, I couldn't breastfeed him, I couldn't care for him as well as I should have because I was so scared and shocked about what was happening. I couldn't make him feel safe, and I couldn't be there 24/7 or make it work with his father so that he had a happy home to come home to. But no matter what I said, Debbie looked at me and said, "It's okay to feel all that, but you're a strong woman. You've been through a lot, and still here you are by your son's side, fighting to be there with him." She then told me a story about something she had read about a little girl who was also in an intensive care unit. Her mom had expressed the same feelings of feeling bad for having to leave her child in the hospital, and that every night she prayed that God would be there in her child's presence when she couldn't, and prayed the angels would be there watching over her child. One day when the little girl was around three years old and at home, after it had stopped raining and there was that fresh scent the rain gives, the little girl said, "Mommy, Mommy, it smells like Him." The mom asked, "Smells like who?" and the little girl replied, "The man that would come play with me in the hospital." The mom smiled and knew immediately whom her daughter was referring to. The story brought a smile to my face. It gave me hope and a positive outlook to think God was with Noah when I couldn't be, that maybe the angels were there surrounding him with their presence and love when I couldn't be. We talked a bit more about everything that was going on with my mom, best friend, and Noah's dad and how I felt. She gave me the best advice and told me that I should focus on two people right now, which were myself and my son. She said, "The rest give to God. There is so much on your plate right now, and you can't take it on all by yourself." I knew she was right. I needed to stop focusing on whether or not my mom was going to help me and my son, whether my best friend was going to be there for me this time, whether my Noah's dad was ever going to want this relationship again or the damage had already been done. After we were done talking and eating lunch, I felt as if I had a boost of strength and courage she provided to me. It was the first time that I didn't feel guilty about having these feelings about my situation, and I no longer beat myself up for having feelings and being human. I knew God was here. He had always been with me since I was a little girl, and I just had to remind myself that He was still here and wouldn't leave my side now that I was in dire need. After meeting with Debbie, I knew it was time for Ryan to be dropping by, so I went back upstairs and said my good-byes to Noah for the day. I decided I finally had some me time and would drive to the old neighborhood I grew up in just to see how much it had changed and to try to reminisce on good memories I had there. I was able to see the house I grew up in and think about being able to bring Noah one day to show him where his mom played as a kid, where she met her best friends as a child, and the after-school program that changed her life. It felt great seeing those things again, some refreshment I needed, going back to where my life had started, all the wonderful things that came with it, and everything I overcame to bring me here to this present moment. After I visited my old home, I went to a restaurant where I often ate as a kid during middle school, a place that brought back the best of memories with my friends, and ordered my favorite meal, which was a cheeseburger with chili- cheese fries. This place was known as Cypress Best, one of the best burger spots in my neighborhood. After spending hours reminiscing, I finally decided to go back to the Ronald McDonald House and catch up on the real world, what was going on with life and the news. After watching the news, it was weird to see everything that was going on. It was as though the world was blowing right past me and I had no idea besides the trouble that was in front of me.

During this time, the Dodgers had gone to the playoffs again and lost to the Washington Nationals. There were so many fires occurring, to the point that it seemed like all of Southern California was on fire. The fire was close to home on the 14 freeway near Acton. It was then I decided it was best I just turned the TV off and went to bed, ready to face the next day head-on.

November 11, 2019

As Monday rolled in, I was so excited. I knew today was the day they were going to try to bottle-feed Noah to see if he had begun swallowing, since he was constantly sucking on his pacifier. The pacifier was Noah's security blanket. He would only stay calm and not cry if it was in his mouth, and he seemed to be swallowing his saliva. Once I was at the hospital, I spotted Diane, and she let me know she was on her way to get the formula and bottle for Noah. I put my things in the locker and headed over to his pod and saw the nurse changing Noah, getting him ready to sit up. I began to talk to Noah, and the nurse informed me today was the big day to see if Noah was ready to finally eat. As Diane walked in, she told me how it was going to go. She would try a preemie nipple to begin, since the other nipples might release a heavier flow. She picked up Noah and placed him in a sitting position and rubbed the bottle nipple on his lips, giving him a drop of formula, which in return he began to smack his lips and taste. His eyes became enlarged, and he began trying to find the nipple. At first, he began to spit up and choke a little, but after several attempts, he latched on to the bottle and drank two milliliters of formula. I was so relieved and happy to see that my son had not lost his sense of knowing what it meant to eat with his mouth again. To see how wide-eyed he was to finally have formula back in his mouth was heartwarming. Diane said she would stop there, since he had choked a bit in the beginning. She stated she wanted to make sure he hadn't aspirated, so she would let the doctor know to do a possible X-ray just to make sure that the formula went down the correct tube and not into his lungs. At that moment, I was so hopeful, just seeing him being able to latch on to the nipple and take down two milliliters of milk. After everything that had happened, Noah was able to go to sleep. At this time, I was trained and allowed to set up G-tube feedings and take his temp. I was no longer afraid, and I told myself that in order to get familiar with how to take care of Noah, I might as well jump in and do what the nurses were doing, which was every three hours change his diaper, take his temperature, set up the formula, and feed him. So I nervously asked the nurse if I could start doing these things, and if she could just supervise to see if I was doing them correctly. I was a first-time mom, and yes, even then, I was still new to changing diapers and taking temperatures under the armpit, so I wanted to make sure I was providing the best care I could for my son. The nurse smiled at me and said of course and began to watch over me as I did everything. She saw me do everything and gave me tips and pointers on how it would be easier to change his diaper by putting a fresh one under so that poop wouldn't get anywhere, and of course packing on the Desitin. After I set up his food, she was amazed at how fast I learned, but I explained to her that I had previous experience with a G-tube, since my cousin had one and I was his caregiver for a while. After my doing everything, she told me she would print out the training sheets and mark off that I had completed the G-tube training, since I was now setting up Noah's formula and the feeding machine to feed him. After the feeding, I held Noah for an hour before I went to pump. It was now evening, and my family was coming to take me out to dinner, since I had finally told them about the split between Noah's dad and me; they just didn't know how bad it was. We went to go eat Thai food, and we were able to get together and laugh and try to be normal. But no matter how much I enjoyed my family's company and reminisced about the past, there was still a constant reminder in my heart that my son was still in the hospital. This had been my home for almost two months now, and there was absolutely nothing I could do besides pray for a miracle, pray for this nightmare to be over so I could go home and hopefully we could be a family again. As I finished dinner, I thanked my family for coming to visit me through this tough time and told them that since I would be at the hospital for Thanksgiving, I planned to stay there with Noah and would not be attending our traditional family dinner. They were saddened by the news but understood and told me they would not be getting together, since it wouldn't be the same without Noah and me present. When I returned to the Ronald McDonald House, I prayed that night as vigorously as I could, praying that Noah could eat again tomorrow. They would try again to feed him until he was able to swallow ten milliliters. They needed him to swallow that amount in order to conduct the swallow test. The next day, I hurried in to ask the nurse if he had gained any weight, so we could be closer to going upstairs to the PICU, and asked what time Diane was coming in to try to feed Noah again. The nurse explained to me that at 6 a.m. they had conducted an X-ray on Noah's chest to make sure he had not aspirated, and that the doctor filling in for his normal doctor (who was on vacation) would be contacted shortly to discuss the results with me. Two minutes later, Dr. B walked in and told me they had performed an X-ray on Noah's chest and found that he had aspirated. She pulled up a picture of the X-ray on the computer and showed me that the fluid was in his lungs. She told me that because of this, Noah would not continue to feed and would have to be administered an IV and placed on antibiotics for seven days for the infection. I was just there in shock, trying to find the right words to say and trying to prevent my knees from giving out from underneath me. I asked her if after the seven days, would he try again to eat? Dr. B stated no, that she would recommend for Noah not to eat until he was a toddler and able to take down thicker foods, like pureed food. I immediately became enraged because I felt as if the doctor was writing off my son because of this. Why couldn't we try again? He once ate for two weeks, so why stop because of one complication? Why kill my hope and tell me to not even try until my son was two to get him to eat? I told the doctor that his G-tube was placed as a precaution due to his trach being placed, not because Noah couldn't eat, so why wouldn't we try again? Could it be the discomfort of swallowing with the trach? Could we first rule out all the things that were riding against Noah? He had just gotten surgery almost two weeks ago and hadn't eaten anything by mouth. But she continued to state that was her recommendation and she would inform OT not to come, and she walked over to the next parents in the room to discuss their child's progress. I wanted to scream and cause a scene, but I figured I'd do what I knew best, and that was rely on God. Science, medicine, and everything else goes by protocol and statistics; however, I knew I believed in a God who created miracles and moved mountains. I would bring this to Him and leave it at His feet instead of taking it as a defeat. The nurse informed me that they would be starting an IV to get the antibiotics running, and that he did have a fever this morning. As I stood there waiting for the nurses to come, I prayed over Noah in hopes they would be able to find a vein right away. When the nurses came in, they brought in a yellow-and-red light and placed it under Noah's hand to try to find a vein on his right hand. A few attempts were made, but they were unable to find a vein. After five minutes of attempting, they called in the charge nurse to try to get his vein. At this point, Noah was crying and had two desaturations due to the pain he was experiencing of getting pricked by a needle over and over again. I continued singing to him "Baby of Mine," trying to distract him as they continued to try to find a vein. I held in my tears, trying not to cry, because I wanted to tell them over and over to stop already. Finally, they were able to find a vein and begin the antibiotics. As soon as he fell asleep, I ran out of there like a bat out of hell. I ran to the restroom and entered the handicap stall and just began crying and crying. Everything hit me all at once—everything the doctor had told me—from Noah being written off to the six minutes of him being pricked over and over. I just sat on the toilet and cried. Finally, someone entered the restroom, so I broke my cry, flushed the toilet, and grabbed my things and headed to the exit. As I went to my car, I tried to wipe the tears off my face, trying to avoid anyone, since my eyes were bloodshot red. I didn't know where to go. I was hungry but didn't want to eat. I felt bad that I couldn't continue to stay by Noah's bedside, so I went to the spot where I felt the most at home, and that was my childhood home. I drove by Avenue 43 and drove to my old house and parked nearby, just remembering all the good times I had as a kid and reminiscing on how I had pictured my life as an adult would be. I never would have thought I would be in a situation like this with a child, let alone one fighting for survival, and trying to save my family. I had to keep reminding myself to focus on the positive and remember that tough little girl who grew up around boys and felt she could take on the world. I remembered a time when my cousin and I built a go-cart out of a power wheel, duct tape, and an old mattress cushion. We would ride down the dirt road, thinking about how invincible and smart we were for taking our very own go-cart for a ride. I remembered that time being one of the most memorable times of my life. I remembered that feeling and wished I had that feeling right now. I began to pray to regain my strength and happiness right now so I could build my strength again to go back and fight. I went back to my car and headed for home, knowing tomorrow was a different day, a new day where I could look forward and remember who I was.

November 15, 2019

Noah was on day seven of his antibiotic, and the nurses informed me they would be taking off the IV. Noah would then be back to normal, and I could resume setting up his feeds and picking him up again. I was finally able to speak to his doctor who had come back from vacation and told her what Dr. B had stated and what I felt about Noah being written off. She informed me that she did not agree with what the acting doctor had stated, especially since Noah had eaten before. She told me, statistically, many trach babies do not like swallowing after a trach being placed, but by muscle memory and constant practice and thickening the milk, it can be done. She informed me she had put in an order for the OT to resume sessions with Noah. The doctor told me that on a positive note, Noah had gained weight, so he was only a few ounces away from going upstairs to the PICU. That morning I saw my brave Noah there in a T-shirt and a beanie I had left; the charge nurse came in and told me she had given Noah a bath and put on the clothes I had left. She told me how much he had laughed and smiled when the water was poured on his head. I told her, "Thank you very much!" I really appreciated her; she always came to check on Noah and would massage him and do little things for him even if she was the charge nurse on duty. She told me she had grown a soft spot for him, since she had been there when they removed him out of the OR and placed him in his pod. I was happy that day; it was little wins like these when I felt a sense of hope and victory in my corner. The nurse also informed me Noah was two ounces away from going upstairs, and they had already informed the PICU to give me a tour of the floor so I would know where everything was located. There was a big possibility we would be upstairs by tomorrow. I received a phone call from the social worker, and she asked me if we could meet after lunch, since she had been informed by the nurse that I needed support or guidance due to everything that was happening with Noah and between me and Noah's dad, and the tension that was being presented by Noah's bedside.

I went to go eat in the cafeteria, and I will admit, I was nervous about talking to a social worker. I didn't know if they would report anything or if it would hinder Noah from being discharged, since they had told us Noah could be discharged only if two people were trained in the same household. I figured this would be an effective way to vent and release all my frustration and concerns, since social workers were there to help, not hurt, families. I knew, due to Noah's dad's past, that if he knew I was speaking to a social worker, he would be livid. However, I knew this was something I had to do for me and my sanity, and of course to get the answers I needed for Noah's sake. I didn't want him to be held in the hospital longer because his parents couldn't keep it together, especially since I had read from the Trach Moms' support group that if you had nowhere to go, then the hospital would not discharge you. After lunch I went to the social worker's office, which was right near the NICU. She introduced herself as Maria and told me she wanted to be a form of support and an ear to hear what was going on, especially with everything I was going through. As I walked into her office, she asked me to sit down and asked me if everything was okay, and just by that question, I immediately broke. I couldn't get one word out without bawling, as though every emotion came running out. After I was able to finally muster out words, I told her that I been going through so much with everything with Noah, and that I was so afraid I was going to fail as his mom because I was so scared to touch his trach. I also explained how I felt overwhelmed by not being home and having to go back and forth between the Ronald McDonald House and the hospital. I told her that after dealing with all this, it had put a wedge between Noah's dad and me, that we were no longer on speaking terms and had created a schedule so we were not both by Noah's bedside at the same time. I told her it had come to a point where I now had to consider what was going to happen when we got discharged. I believed we would no longer be together, which scared me because all of my and Noah's stuff was at the apartment, and I would have to take time to stop everything and transition everything to my mom's house. I also asked if this would change anything about Noah's discharge, if his dad and I were to separate. She told me that it might because the child must be released to a household where two individuals were trained and able to fully take care of Noah. She asked if there might be anyone else I could have come in and train, such as my mom, since I would be living with her. I sat there and thought about it for a minute and responded with, "I will ask her." She asked me if there was any way I believed Noah's dad and I would be able to settle our differences and discuss the future. She mentioned that she knew how stressful this was and the toll it could take on individuals, and she said sometimes we release that stress and anger on those closest to us. I sat there and heard her out and agreed. I knew we were having difficulty managing our stress, dealing with what had occurred, while trying to save our relationship. We both had not envisioned this occurring; we had thought we would be home with our little boy three days later, living the ever-after dream. Being first-time parents, we had no idea what we were up against. I thanked the social worker for listening to me. She told me to let her know if I needed anything and said, as of right now, if I could have a backup plan by getting my mom down here to learn the training, that would be great. As I left her office, I felt so much better, like a rock had been lifted off my shoulder. I went to the NICU to see Noah, and he was there staring at his mobile, smiling once he heard my voice. I told him how proud I was of him, and how strong and brave he was for overcoming the pneumonia and gaining weight in all this matter to move on to the next step to discharge. I was able to see the nurse remove both IVs from Noah's hand and foot. I kissed his wounds and held him again for hours. The charge nurse came over and checked on Noah and told me they had informed the PICU that more than likely, tomorrow he would be placed in the PICU. Shortly after, Diane, the OT, walked in and informed me she had received the new orders from the doctor to try feeding again. She told me that since Noah seemed to aspirate, she was going to start baby steps with him and just try to dip a pacifier in the breast milk I provided or in the formula and give it to him to see if he would swallow. She had a nurse bring formula, and we both tried it together. We were able to see Noah latch on to the pacifier and suck on the pacifier vigorously. She told me she would do this with him as much as she could until she saw he could swallow more, and then she would transition to bottle-feeding. I was so happy. My son was going to be able to hopefully swallow, and most importantly, he was not going to be written off. As it became evening, I knew we had another training on how to clean the trach once it was removed, since we would have to replace it weekly. The nurse called a respiratory therapist (RT) in so we could get the stuff ready to do the trach care.

When Noah's dad arrived after work, he would be the leader this time, since I had completed all my training. Once Noah's dad arrived, the RT came in and showed us how to scrub the trach properly with a trach-care kit and told us to make sure everything was sterile, since we would probably have to reuse the trach, depending on how many trachs the insurance sent each month. Afterward, Noah's dad set up the trach care and we started. For the first time, we didn't fight. We listened to the RT's advice, and he told us it might seem scary and tough, but we had to remember that if the trach popped out, we could just put it back in with the spare trach that should always be placed by Noah's bedside. The RT told us something that made everything seem less scary and put us both on a calmer level rather than us panicking and becoming unraveled. He stated, "Remember, guys, Noah can breathe. He needs the trach only because of his apnea when he goes to sleep, so if the trach pops out, it is okay. Remain calm; Noah is still breathing. It will take some time for him to adjust off the vent, but you have to remember that Noah can breathe while he is awake and won't stop breathing if it pops out." Once he said that, it was like something clicked in both of our minds. We had been so afraid to let the trach pop out because we were afraid Noah wouldn't be able to breathe, but we realized that there was no reason to panic. That day was the first time that we were able to effectively communicate as a team. Everything went smoothly with his trach care, and for some reason, Noah was calm. I assumed it was because for the first time, there was no tension and he wasn't hearing his parents yell at each other. But whatever it was, we finally were able to complete the trach care without getting mad at each other, and both of our trainings were now complete. I was gathering my stuff to head out to give Noah's dad some alone time with Noah. He asked me if I was going to get dinner, because he was hungry. I told him yes, and he asked if I wanted to get food together. As we left the hospital, we decided to grab pizza and go to a nearby restaurant. As we sat there, at first we were both quiet. Noah's dad broke the ice by saying how great of a job we had done during trach care, and that hopefully we could continue on the same path. I told him that I knew we had been acting like enemies instead of like partners, but we needed to work together in order to make sure Noah came home. I told him that it wasn't fair to Noah; he needed two parents as strong as ever to help him through this, not two parents bickering. Noah's dad agreed, and

I asked him if we could try one more time for Noah's sake to try to make it work and be the better version of ourselves. He told me he wanted to think about it because he didn't want to ruin anything, and that he wanted the same thing for Noah, but we couldn't see eye to eye on things. I felt a stab in the chest, that even though I was willing to try to work this out, despite his lack of support and belittlements, he still needed time to think about it. At this point, I just agreed, and after dinner I went back to the room while he went back to see Noah. I was drowning in my negative thoughts, even feeling the ugliest, since my C-section pouch seemed to be bigger. Looking in the mirror after a shower, I realized how much my body had changed. I was cleared to start working out, but I had no time or energy to do anything. I had to fight away the thoughts and tell myself over and over that tomorrow was going to be a great day. Noah was going to continue to have OT, we had finished our training, and hopefully tomorrow he would be in the PICU. I went to sleep listening to worship music, and it just so happened "You Make Me Brave" came on the station. I knew right then and there that God was telling me He was still here and He hadn't forgotten about me.

November 18, 2019

I woke up really early, full of excitement, hoping today would be the day we went up to the PICU. Noah needed only two more ounces to reach eight pounds, and then we could start making plans to get back home where we belonged. As I headed to get breakfast at McDonald's, I started to look around and noticed all the Christmas decorations people were putting up in the neighborhood, and realized Christmas was around the corner. I also realized that Thanksgiving was that following Thursday, and I had no idea where we would be or what we would be doing. As I entered the hospital, I went straight to the NICU. As I walked in, the nurse beamed with a big smile, and the doctor stated to me Noah finally did it. He was eight pounds, four ounces, and my heart smiled. I knew today was the big day. The nurse informed me the PICU was aware Noah would be going upstairs. I was so excited. I didn't know what would happen next, but I knew we were one step closer to going home. As Noah lay asleep, I stepped outside to tell Noah's dad the good news, and he was as excited as I was. I went back inside the room, and the nurse told me to start gathering his things by the crib and anything else that I needed to take upstairs with me. I gathered my things, kissed Noah, and told him the exciting news. Shortly after, a nurse came from upstairs and told us she would be our nurse for the day in the PICU, and that as soon as a respiratory therapist came to assist her, they would be wheeling up Noah in his crib to his room. I asked the nurse if I would be able to spend the night in the room with him, and she said of course. As the day turned to evening, I hurried back to the Ronald McDonald House to pick up some food and pack a bag to sleep over. I also picked up Noah's diaper bag. It was untouched, since he hardly wore clothes because of the trach and heat sensitivity. I hoped that by bringing the diaper bag, I would finally be able to dress up Noah and have some private time with him without other families present or six other nurses in and out of the room. As I hurried back to the NICU to make sure I didn't miss the transfer, I ran into the charge nurse. She told me how happy she was to learn that Noah was finally going up to the PICU, and that she would make sure to go up and visit us. I hurried into Noah's pod and saw that the respiratory therapist was there, removing the wiring from Noah so he could be wheeled up in his crib. As I gathered the rest of the things and sat there, doctors came over and wished us luck and hoped we would be on our way home soon. Every nurse and respiratory therapist who had taken care of Noah came over to say their good-byes, and I was touched to know how many people had been impacted by Noah's soft smile and long hair. They told me stories of what they had experienced with him, and NICU staff knew him as "Noah with the hair," since his hair was exceptionally long and beautiful. As I looked across the room, I noticed a mother there in the corner with her head down, crying. I knew her son had been there the same amount of time Noah had, but I didn't know her story or her baby's condition. I just knew by the doctor's visits and the desaturations, it wasn't looking as if she would be going home anytime soon. As I sat there happy, smiling as they told me we were almost ready to go (we were waiting for the call from the PICU, and then we would be on our way), I tried my best to smile, but it hurt my heart to see the mom in the corner crying. I had been there, trying to be happy for the other moms who were leaving but feeling sad about my situation, how my baby and I would not be going anywhere. No matter how much you had to brave a strong face, it hurt like hell. I didn't know how many moms before me she had to see leave, but I wanted to walk over there and say, "Everything is going to be okay. I was once there where you were, and your time will come. Please do not give up hope, and I'm praying for you." Just as I was building up courage to go over there, we received the call, so I quietly said a prayer for her and her child, that they would be home soon. The nurse told me they were ready for us, and we started to wheel Noah out straight upstairs to the PICU. We waved good-bye to everyone, including the receptionist in the front, who seemed to give me a smile of encouragement. She told me, "Take care and God bless," and we left. As we arrived in the PICU, we walked straight into Noah's room, where they had stationed his crib in one corner. Next to his bed were a sink and a cabinet where we could hang his clothes or our clothes if we stayed over. Next to his bed was a couch, which pulled out as a bed so we could spend the night, and another dresser area to put our things. The best part was it had a big window where we could view the city, and two comfortable chairs to sit in. It was only the two of us in the room, and the nurse informed us that in the PICU, the nurse would come in and out to check on Noah, but I could close the glass sliding door for privacy. I was so relieved. Finally, I could have privacy with my son, have our own room where I could finally sleep next to him, and, most importantly, where I could do everything as if I were home and it were just he and I. The nurse showed me where the showers were, if I wanted to shower in the morning. She also let me know that the cafeteria allowed breakfast, lunch, and dinner for the parents who were staying in the room, and I could have up to five people in the room to visit Noah. That night I changed and got into my pajamas and pulled out the bed. I didn't know what to do. I felt so anxious. Should I sit and watch him sleep? Should I try to go to bed and get some rest, knowing that I was in the same room as Noah? I did what I normally did in the NICU: I sat right by his bed, singing him his lullabies, running my fingers through his hair as he went to sleep. The night shift took over, and the night nurse and respiratory therapist came in and introduced themselves. They informed me that they would be coming in when it was feeding time to check him, feed him, change his diaper, and check his vitals, and would be changing his ties right before bed. I asked them if I could do it, since I had been doing it in the NICU, but they said they would do it the first night, and tomorrow I could start throughout the day. As Noah went to sleep and they checked him and set up his feed, the nurse told me to go to bed. I tried my best to lie down and doze off, but any little movement Noah did, I would jump out of bed and run toward him to let him know I was there and he wasn't alone. Once he went back to sleep, I lay down, and shortly after, the nurse and respiratory therapist came in and out to change him, feed him, and change his ties. It was now 12:30 a.m., and my son was up crying because he wanted to be left alone. That night was rough for both of us. I stayed up watching from the corner of the room while they changed his ties. Just to be more specific, when Noah cried, you could not hear noise from him. The only way to know was by hearing the machines going off because he was holding his breath, mad and desaturating, or his heart rate was high. Without the monitors, you would have been unable to know there was a baby present in the room. As I stood there watching, I saw Noah desaturating and kicking and fighting while the ties were trying to be changed. They asked me if he was normally like that, and I told them yes, because he was unfamiliar with them. When his dad or I changed them, he was calmer. Once everything was over, Noah settled down and went back to sleep. Every three hours, they came in again to set up his feed, and at 6 a.m., the next shift took over. By 7 a.m., everyone was making their rounds and having meetings outside each patient's room. A team meeting was held to go over what had happened throughout the night and discuss how the patient was doing. That night I learned that I wouldn't be able to get much sleep because of the constant in and out, Noah's crying, and having to get up early to be part of the team debriefing. In the NICU, parents had to leave for this, so only staff personnel discussed the patient; but in the PICU, the parents were welcome to join, in case they wanted to hear the status or be updated with anything new that might be happening with their child's plan of care. That day, I knew it was a victory; we would be discussing Noah's plan of care and possible discharge date. During rounds that morning, the doctors, nurses, and respiratory therapists huddled together and began going over Noah's case right outside the door. After going over the diagnosis, the doctor told me they would be removing the hospital ventilator and putting him on a home ventilator, an Astral 150, which was the same one he would be going home with, to see if he was able to remain stable. I asked if we would finally be able to receive a possible discharge date. The doctor told me they would have to give Noah a few weeks on the ventilator to make sure there were no desaturations, but they were hoping soon. I was happy with any mention of a discharge date. Just hearing it was in the near future brightened my day. After the meeting, a doctor walked in whom I had never seen before and introduced himself as the geneticist doctor. He wanted to discuss a few things with me. He began stating that he had looked over Noah's chart, and after examining him, he believed Noah had a rare genetic syndrome called Joubert syndrome. He asked me if Noah's dad and I could get our blood drawn in order to see if this was in fact the syndrome. He said it could be the reason for the respiratory issues, and Noah had all the characteristics of it, such as droopy eyes, low ears, and arched eyebrows. He continued to tell me not to look up or google information until we got the results, especially since the Internet shows the worst-case scenario. He ended the conversation by stating once we knew the diagnosis, then we could come up with a plan of action for Noah and know more of a prognosis for him. I just nodded and tried not to be sad on such a victorious day. That same afternoon, Noah's dad and I went to get our blood drawn. On the walk over there, I began to cry. I had looked up Joubert syndrome and seen the worst of the worst. It mentioned that kids with this syndrome might not walk and might have cognitive delays. They could have lifelong respiratory issues, as well as liver and kidney failure, which could lead to death. I couldn't wrap my brain around everything, and reading articles just made me cry. After the blood draw, I went back to the Ronald McDonald House, while Noah's dad went to the hospital to spend the night with Noah. I told him I wanted to be alone that night and just sleep, but I would be there the next morning. Noah's dad told me not to worry, that this might not even be the syndrome, and they were still trying to figure everything out. I told him I just wanted to rest. As I entered the room, I called my mom and told her everything. I just cried and told her to pray and hope Noah didn't have this rare genetic syndrome. I texted my family in a group message, updating them about what had occurred all in one day and asked for all the prayers I could get. I lay down hoping I would wake up from this nightmare. The next morning, I pumped and continued on my way to the hospital. I was still trying to produce as much milk as I could, but it was very little. I entered the PICU and went into Noah's room and saw Noah and his dad asleep.

I pulled up a chair next to Noah's crib and just watched him while he slept. Shortly after, the nurse came in and informed me Noah was on the home ventilator and had been doing good on it with no desaturations, which was great. She told me the pulmonologist would be dropping by to go over everything regarding the home ventilator and the process toward discharge. Around 10 a.m., the pulmonologist stepped in and told me Noah had been on the home ventilator since last night and there had been no desaturations. He told me this was great news because usually babies take weeks to adjust to the ventilator, which was why they must observe them. I asked what the difference was between the hospital ventilator and the home vent, and he stated it was the pressure. He continued to state that with Noah doing such an excellent job, he might be able to go home sooner than we anticipated, and I smiled. I just thanked God. I knew my boy was strong, but I knew God was working behind all this. I knew He had been with Noah all along. The doctor told me he would check in next week to see how Noah was doing, and we would go from there. The doctor stated that as of right now, they had Noah's discharge date for December 15. I said, "Thank You, Jesus!" and thanked the doctor. We were finally seeing a light at the end of the tunnel. The doctor told me that usually trach babies stayed for around six months or longer, but Noah was proving us wrong and wanting to get out of here fast as well. I smiled. My son was so strong through all this; he still held a smile and seemed happy despite his circumstances. As the doctor walked out, I immediately starting crying and hugged Noah. I continued to pray and thank God for being with us and getting us closer to home. I began to kiss Noah's forehead and tell him he did it; he was so strong and brave, and he did it—we were going home soon.

Around 2 p.m., Noah's dad and I decided to go out to eat just to get away for a bit. We informed the nurse, and she told us to stay out long and take some time for ourselves, which we knew would only be a couple of hours, since we always rushed back. As we were driving to the restaurant, I received a phone call from the geneticist. The geneticist started off by stating the blood results had come back, and after thoroughly looking over all the chromosomes, they had determined it was Joubert syndrome. He explained that in my blood I had half of a chromosome known as CSPP1, and Noah's dad had the other half, so when we came together, we gave Noah the full chromosome.

He asked whether any of our families had Jewish or German in their bloodline. I stated Noah's dad did; however, as far as I knew, I was full Mexican, so I had no idea how I had that. He stated that since we now had a diagnosis to tie with Noah's condition, we could go over a proper plan of care and what to expect. He stated he would stop by tomorrow to go over everything and inform the doctor of what he had found. Everything was like a blur to me. I asked a question, such as, Could Noah beat this? I was not thinking of course, and he said unfortunately, because it was a genetic syndrome, there was no changing it; it was part of his DNA. All we could do was watch and observe him and go over worst- and best-case scenarios for Noah. I held back tears and told him I would see him tomorrow. I hung up the phone, looked at Noah's dad, and sobbed. There were only negative thoughts in my mind at this time. We gave this to him—it was our fault. How was this possible? Only 1 in 100,000 around the world, and we were that one. I knew it was wrong of me to do so, but the guilt overrode everything positive I had been feeling. All I could do was blame myself. Noah's dad held me and fought back tears too. He felt the same pain—it was our coming together that gave Noah this. Who would have thought? We both lost our appetite because of this news. Both of us had been hopeful that Noah wouldn't have this disorder, and I felt knocked down again. What I had read about this syndrome wasn't good, and most importantly, it was rare that articles didn't provide answers to anything. It was more of scenarios and just observing your child as he or she became older. We went back to the room and just picked up food along the way, not talking. As soon as we arrived at the Ronald McDonald House, we ate, and I told Noah's dad I would be going to sleep while he went to go tuck Noah into bed. I didn't have the strength to go back, and it killed me. I could now sleep at the PICU with my son, but I was choosing to stay in the room because I was so exhausted. I was failing as a mom, and I let the negative thoughts consume me as I went to bed.

November 22, 2019—Thanksgiving

At this point in time, Noah's dad and I were no longer on speaking terms. He found out that I had talked to a social worker, since the social worker wanted to discuss things with him so we could all be on the same page. He told me he could does not trust me anymore and didn't want to work anything out, since he felt I went behind his back to discuss things with a social worker. I told him I had no choice, that I needed to figure out if Noah's discharge date would change if he was going home with only me. He continued to state that he would never allow me to take his son away, and I just left it at that. That morning when I walked into the hospital, I put Noah's turkey onesie on and took pictures with him at the bedside. I told myself I was going to have a good day today no matter how bad I felt. We were stuck spending our first Thanksgiving in a hospital away from our family. However, I remained positive, held Noah, and told him "Happy Thanksgiving" while he slept. I told him we would get a redo next year, where we would be surrounded by our family, filled with love and laughter. I put on the TV for him so he could have some noise in the background. The only children's channel that worked was Nickelodeon, and we watched SpongeBob together. Shortly after, Noah's dad stopped by, and I began gathering my things so I could head out so we wouldn't be in the same room together. However, he told me I could stay, that I didn't have to leave, and asked me how Noah was doing. I told him Noah was good and he had just been relaxing. The nurse dropped in and told us "Happy Thanksgiving" and asked how we were and what our plans were for the day. She urged us to go out and grab some food while Noah slept. I'll never forget, it was a rainy day that holiday, and for the first time in years, it was snowing back in our town, Lancaster. Once the nurse stepped out, Noah's dad asked me if I wanted to go have a Thanksgiving dinner so at least we could feel a little better. I agreed, and we looked up restaurants that were open, since everything seemed closed due to the holiday. We ended up going to Sizzler, which was one of my favorite childhood restaurants, and it was the same one I had frequented as a kid. We ordered the salad bar and sat down; it was as crowded as I expected, but there were a lot of families there celebrating the holiday. During dinner Noah's dad brought up the social worker again, and I told him why I had done it. He said he wanted to move forward and work things out, but without the social worker involved. He continued to state he felt we would have bad days, but he wanted to try to make this work and wanted Noah to go back to our home where we could raise him together. It was everything I wanted to hear at that time. I had been raised in a broken house without a father, and it was my dream to have my little family together. I especially wanted Noah to have a father, which is something I longed for as a kid, and I didn't want Noah to suffer as I did. As we made our way back to the hospital, we talked about things we still needed to complete back at the apartment, such as cleaning and making sure we had enough room for all of Noah's equipment that would be coming home with us. As we arrived at the hospital, I asked the nurse if I could hold Noah. She handed me to him with all his wires, and I put the Boppy around my waist for arm support and rocked Noah in my arms. After an hour of my holding him, Noah's dad asked if he could hold him. I agreed and stood up with him while Noah's dad became situated in the chair. I began to hand him Noah, and the wires became tangled. He began raising his voice at me, telling me I was doing it all wrong and Noah was all tangled up now because of me. I told him to lower his voice, since he was being loud and Noah was beginning to cry, but he continued to be loud and yell for me to help him untangle the wires. The nurse overheard the commotion and walked in, asking if we needed help. Noah's dad continued to state no, we were fine. As soon as she left, he began raising his voice again, stating I didn't help him and it was ridiculous. I began to tell him not to talk to me like that, and he told me I never help him with Noah and why he wasn't in love with me anymore. I stood there frozen. I couldn't believe he told me that, and it felt like a knife stabbing my chest. At this point, I picked up my things and walked out. I went straight to the Ronald McDonald House and changed and just lay there holding my chest. This was the first time Noah's dad had mentioned he didn't love me, and it made me feel that everything was a lie. We had just finished talking about putting the past behind us and working this out so we could be a family for Noah. At this point, I told myself I wasn't going to care anymore. It was about bringing Noah home, and that was all I was going to be focused on.

December 2, 2019

That morning as I was getting ready for the day, a nurse came in and informed me that due to the granulomas that had formed around Noah's trach, they would have to take pictures and notify the ENT, since they were excessively big. Around 10 a.m., the ENT called me and informed me they would recommend a silver nitrate procedure. The doctor explained how the procedure would go and informed me it was a Q-tip with silver nitrate on it that would be used to rub on the granulomas so they could burn off to prevent the granulomas from blocking the trach hole. I asked, "Will the procedure hurt?" The doctor explained to me that since a granuloma is dead skin, it would only burn a little and the area would be irritated, but Noah could be given Tylenol for any discomfort. Even though I didn't want to put Noah through another hurtful procedure, I felt it sounded drastic but something that needed to be done in order to prevent any blockage near his stoma (trach site). I was dreading this once again. However, I didn't know anything about granulomas at the time, so I agreed to do the procedure, since it sounded like something Noah was in dire need of. The doctor informed me the procedure would be at 2 p.m., and they would go over everything with me again once they arrived. I was honestly scared; I didn't know what would happen. The fact that my son was barely two months old and was having his skin burned off his neck made me feel helpless again. I didn't want him to have any more pain. No more being in the hospital, no more pokes—that was the only thing I wanted for Noah. However, I knew I had to think positive, so I thought, *What would be in the best interest for Noah?* I continued to ask myself what Jesus would do? From the looks of it, it sounded as if the procedure would help him. I prayed for comfort for Noah, for it to be quick, and of course for it to be pain free. At 1 p.m., I was anxiously waiting for the doctor to come. I figured I would do my best to try to calm my nerves and calm Noah, so I began to sing songs to him. I turned on his favorite playlist, which was Mickey's favorite hits, and we put on "Old McDonald," and he began smiling and laughing, holding on to my finger. I pretended to clap his hands together while we continued to sing his favorite songs, such as "Green Grass Grows All Around," and "Twinkle, Twinkle, Little Star." I played with his hair and explained to him what was going to happen, hoping he would understand. Around 2 p.m., the doctor arrived and informed me he would be filling in for Dr. N, since she was in the surgery room. He explained to me how the procedure would be conducted and showed me the tube carrying the silver nitrate. The doctor discussed with me that the ties should be changed twice a day, at night and in the morning, since some of the silver nitrate residue might be exposed to the ties and gauze. Shortly after, the respiratory therapist and nurse walked in to assist with the procedure. The procedure was going to be done at his bedside, since it was just a matter of placing the silver nitrate on the granulomas. They began positioning the bed and swaddling him, since they knew he would kick and fight during the procedure. I stepped back as soon as they began swaddling him, and he began crying and desaturating. It broke my heart to see how traumatized he was and how he knew being swaddled meant something terrible was going to happen. I couldn't stand there and watch. I wanted to scream and tell them to leave him alone, to forget the procedure and let it be. But I knew he needed this, since the granulomas were big enough to cover the trach hole. As my emotions overcame me, I stepped out of the room, holding back tears, and looked away as the procedure began. I cried while looking away. I cried because my son was yet again going through another painful procedure. I cried for feeling so guilty, knowing I couldn't be a strong enough mother to hold his hand during the procedure. I was too mentally and emotionally weak to sit in during the procedure. I felt as if I had abandoned him when he needed his mom, or to at least let him know someone was there for him. However, I couldn't do it. I knew at that very moment I would never forgive myself. Ten minutes later, the procedure was over. The doctor walked out of the room and told me he had informed the respiratory therapist and nurse on how to take care of the trach site. I told him thank you and walked back into the room. I saw Noah there asleep, drained from all the kicking and desaturation that had occurred during the procedure. I asked the nurse if Noah could please receive Tylenol for his pain and asked at what time the trach ties and gauze would be changed, since they looked like a light gray due to the silver nitrate. She informed me that the trach care would occur once the night shift arrived at seven, since they had been changed prior to the procedure. As they left, I sat next to Noah's bed and began crying and apologizing to him over and over. "I'm sorry I couldn't be there holding your hand. I'm sorry I was too emotionally and mentally weak to be by your side." The guilt and my self-worth weighed so heavily on me that I completely felt as though I had failed him. I began feeling that if he knew the truth when he was older, he wouldn't be able to forgive me. I knew, of course, he wouldn't remember firsthand, but if he knew the truth, I questioned if he would be okay with it. I begged and prayed for God to forgive me for not being brave enough and to get all the negative thoughts out of my head. I kissed Noah and hummed him his lullabies and noticed his heart rate was very high. I called for the nurse to give him Tylenol due to the pain. I stayed there until the evening, and I was exhausted. I informed the nurse that I was headed to dinner and would be back later. I ate food back at the Ronald McDonald House, then decided to go lie down. As I closed my eyes, I was awoken by Noah's dad, who had told me he was going to go visit Noah at the hospital and wish him a good night, and asked if I was going to sleep over at the PICU. I told him I was too tired to move, so I was going to sleep and would head there first thing in the morning. The next day at 4 a.m., I woke up startled and mad at myself for not having the strength to get up and go back to the PICU. I kept thinking, *How could I have let him sleep alone?* So I hurried, got ready, and went straight to the PICU. I arrived there around 5 a.m. Once I arrived, a nurse was standing over Noah's crib, rocking it back and forth for comfort. I walked in and told the nurse I was here and asked how he had been all night. He told me Noah had been fussy and crying all night, and nothing seemed to calm him besides rocking his crib. I noticed his heart rate was elevated again and asked the nurse if they could please give him Tylenol. I asked if his ties had been changed, since I noticed his gauze was fully gray and the ties looked drenched in sweat, and loose. The nurse informed me they hadn't been changed due to them being busy and said that the morning shift would make sure to do the trach care. As I sat there watching Noah sleep, I examined the gauze. It looked fully gray, which scared me because it was nothing like I had ever seen. Even his skin was gray and discolored. I was really anxious about getting his ties changed, since the ENT had stated they should be changed in the evening. However, I figured it was normal to look gray, since no one seemed concerned regarding the ties not being changed. Throughout the day, Noah seemed to be in a grumpy mood. He couldn't get comfortable and was in and out of sleep, crying. Around 8 a.m., the nurse walked in again and went over Noah's night with me. She said it had not been a good night for him, and he had two desaturations and stayed up most of the night. I told her I wanted an RT to come so we could change the ties, since they were not changed overnight. Shortly after, the respiratory therapist came in and prepared the trach-care supplies while I began to swaddle Noah. I wrapped him in an extra swaddle, since I knew he was already irritable and seemed to be in pain. Once I began swaddling him, it was as if he knew something bad was coming next, so he began crying. I began to sing to him to try to comfort him, but nothing seemed to work. I hated to admit it, but for a typical baby, being swaddled in a blanket meant comfort, while to Noah it meant agony and pain. I stood on his left side and the RT stood on the right side of the crib, and we began to do the trach care. I untied the left side and noticed his neck area was a light gray and looked like it was peeling. As I got the new gauze and dipped it in sterile water to dab the left side of Noah's neck, his skin began to peel off, which exposed bright-red raw skin. Noah began crying, and I immediately became scared and asked the RT to look at his neck. She came around the crib and saw Noah's raw skin. She dabbed his skin with the gauze herself and saw his skin peeling off as well. She became concerned and told me to leave the skin alone and to replace the gauze and tie. During this process, Noah began desaturating, so the RT bumped up his oxygen level to make sure his oxygen didn't drop too low. As soon as we were done, Noah stopped crying, but his heart rate was elevated to 170. The RT told me she would note in his chart that the skin was red and raw. I was really concerned and worried about what I saw, so I immediately called my sister-in-law and told her everything. It was like a burn mark I had seen in a war movie, where the skin just kept peeling, exposing bright-red raw skin. I was hoping it wasn't burned, but when I spoke to my sister-in-law, she said it seemed as if it was a burn. I kissed Noah as he slept and went to the cafeteria to try to take my mind off what I had just witnessed. I informed Noah's dad and told him they were letting the doctor know about his neck. At 2 p.m., I went back to the PICU and saw Noah's nurse by his crib trying to calm him while he was crying. I asked if everything was okay, and the nurse informed me, he had been irritable all morning. I asked him if Noah could please get Tylenol if he hadn't received it yet. I went over to Noah and kissed his forehead and began to sing my own made-up song that I would sing to him for comfort: "Momma's here, Momma's here, Noah's okay, Noah's okay." He opened his eyes to look at me, and I smiled and continued singing. I began to try to explain to him what was happening and what we would be doing for the rest of the day. I began to praise him for being so strong and brave even though he was probably facing the toughest thing in his life. I grabbed the books I had there and began to read to him until he fell asleep. Around 5 p.m., the resident doctor walked in to speak with me. She informed me they were going to do rounds around noon. She also went over his increased desaturations and informed me that they had spoken with pulmonology so they could see him, since his desaturations had increased. She also mentioned they were informed of the redness around the neck area and trach site. I informed her of what I had seen and stated I was concerned because it looked like a burn mark, and I had never seen anything like that. She informed me they discussed it and said it was normal, and anytime silver nitrate is used in a procedure, the area usually becomes red and irritated. I trusted in what she said, since they were the professionals, and hoped it would heal and go away soon. As the day continued, Noah seemed to stay asleep all day, so I pulled the Bible out and began to read. Since Noah was not doing well and seemed more upset as of lately, I told myself I was going to stay with him for the remaining days we had here. According to the hospital, we only had two weeks until discharge, so I knew we were almost out and wanted to get used to having him 24/7. That night I stayed up watching him. He was in and out of sleep and would cry into a desaturation, where I would have to stimulate him due to him turning purple and clamping down. Around 12 a.m., the RT agreed to give Noah one liter of oxygen to help him with his desaturations, since he seemed fussier than usual.

In the morning, the nurse came on shift and debriefed with the night nurse and informed the RT to come to do the morning trach care. Around late afternoon, the RT came in and discussed setting up the trach-care supplies. As soon as we swaddled Noah again, he began kicking and screaming. The nurse held his hands down while I began to loosen the trach tie. During the trach care, I was standing on Noah's right side, which was on the opposite side of the wound area. As soon as I cleaned the right side and it was the RT's turn to clean the left side, the RT looked concerned, and he asked if I had seen the area. I said yes, that I had notified the doctor and nurse two days ago when I first saw it. He then said no, it didn't look right, and informed the nurse to take a picture of the wound and inform the acting PICU doctor on what was occurring. The nurse came in and took a picture and uploaded it to Noah's chart. The RT and nurse said they had never seen anything like it, and they would make sure to notify the doctor and the team. The RT instructed the nurse and me not to rub the area while cleaning Noah's neck. However, the tie still rubbed on it, which was my concern. How would his neck heal when there was a rough-material trach tie around his neck, rubbing every time he moved? The nurse put a soft fabric around his neck to try to prevent any rubbing of the tie. The RT expressed how sorry he was and didn't know why it hadn't been addressed. Shortly after, the doctor walked in and told me she forwarded the picture to the wound-care specialist, and he would be able to come first thing in the morning. I asked the doctor why it hadn't been noted in his chart and discussed earlier, since I had told them two nights ago that Noah's neck was red and peeling. I also told the doctor it had been two nights and two days in which RTs and nurses saw it, but it wasn't until an RT who knew Noah said something was wrong and to take a picture of the wound that it was now being addressed. She told me she needed to go over his chart to see if anything had been reported, but as far as she knew, there were only reports of redness, but nothing of this manner. I became furious. I wanted to scream and yell, blame someone for what was occurring. I hadn't known how bad it was, but I knew my son was in pain. I knew something was wrong with him, and for the medical staff, it seemed they had no idea what was going on. I prayed to God to humble my heart to help me fight this battle, because the words I wanted to use at that moment were not respectful. That night I cried my eyes out. I didn't know what to do or how to protect my son; I felt so lost. I stayed with Noah, hardly sleeping because I was in such a dark place. Noah's dad and I took turns watching Noah to make sure he wasn't in unnecessary discomfort and to make sure he was receiving Tylenol around the clock, since he still seemed agitated.

The next morning, my mom came by at 6 a.m. to take me to Denny's to eat breakfast. I hadn't yet told my family what was occurring, since I wanted to find out what was really going on before I had to explain another situation. At Denny's my mom informed me that she wanted to take me away from the hospital to do my nails. However, I told her I couldn't leave, and she became upset and began to tell me she had come all the way down here for me, and she had already made a nail appointment for me, and she was going to look bad because it was so last minute to cancel. I told her Noah was more important, and I needed to be with him right now. I asked her if she could stay with me at the hospital so she could see Noah and we could eat lunch together. In my time of need, my mom responded with, "I am not canceling my appointment. I need to go do my nails, and I don't like eating the cafeteria food." I was so hurt and furious because I needed my mom and she made everything about her. Little did she know what was occurring at the hospital with Noah or how I was going to have to complain to the doctor about what had occurred. I had her drop me off at the hospital and headed straight to the PICU. Once there I woke Noah's dad and told him rounds were going to start. I was ready to find out what was happening. I was so livid once I was there at the hospital; I was ready to ask questions, ready to find out what had happened, and, most importantly, find out why this had happened to my son. The main doctor, nurses, and RT rounded up around the room, and the main doctor began speaking. He looked at me and said, "The team has been informed about what occurred last night. We sent the picture to the wound doctor, and he stated those are second-degree burns from the silver nitrate; and he will be stopping by in the next thirty minutes to instruct the team as well as you on how to care for the wound." As the doctor said that, I immediately began to cry. I told them how angry I was that my son had second-degree burns, and why. I told them the gauze wasn't changed that night, which had been instructed by the ENT to do. What was the reason this happened? How could this occur? I went on to tell them my son was in pain and crying, and everyone said it was because he was angry, but it was because he had burns around his neck. I told them I had informed the acting resident doctor at the time, and she said it was normal for redness to occur, without checking his neck. Nurses and RTs completed his trach care along with me and saw the wound, but no one reported it until last night when an RT who knew Noah dropped everything and made sure to report it. Could anyone explain to me how this had happened? Everyone in the group had their head down. The acting doctor apologized and said he would call the department administrator (DA) to go over everything with me and make sure to answer my questions; then they left the room. That day I had so much guilt. I sat there with Noah and did everything to hold back my tears and not cry. My son had suffered second-degree burns on his neck and was constantly crying, and I had no idea why. I held his hand and sang "You Are My Sunshine" and told him I would never leave him again. Every night spent in the hospital, he would never be alone; I would always be there in every procedure. Even if I had to suck it up and watch everything while they held him down or stuck him with a needle, I would be right there holding his hand. I knew from then on out that this was a battle I had to face. I would have to be my son's advocate for the rest of his life, since I felt even medical professionals did not seek my son's best interests. I would have to battle doctors, therapists, and nurses in order to receive the best treatment for Noah. I couldn't trust specialists anymore or medical personnel to provide the best care for my son; it had to be me making the final decisions and seeking answers regarding his care and syndrome. I talked to Noah's dad, and we wrote down a plan of action and what questions we would ask when the department administrator came in to speak with us. I wanted to decompress. Noah's dad and I weren't on the best of terms, so we stayed away from each other as much as we could. I went to a taco stand and ate by myself and began to dissect my life. I couldn't believe I was here. I held back my tears and ate and tried to compose myself. Noah's dad called me on the phone and was upset because I left to go eat by myself, and again we began to fight. He began to state that I didn't listen to him and I was inconsiderate. He never seemed to understand my pain, and I didn't understand his. But I didn't care to fight, so I just let him scream and yell while I sat there completely numb. The next morning, the department administrator came into the room, and I began to voice my concerns and questions. She told me she would call the ombudsman to come in and also speak with me so a meeting could take place. Noah seemed better today. I was so afraid to move him around because of the wound on his neck, so I set up his iPad and turned on the movie *Coco* for him. We watched the movie together while I massaged his whole body with lotion and did exercises to try to relax him the best I could. That day we also read his favorite books, sang his favorite songs, and gave him a bed bath. I tried my very best to console him and make him feel safe and comfortable despite our current situation. When the evening came and Noah's dad arrived, we talked. He told me he wanted to be on the same page, especially since we were going to have a meeting with the DA to try to figure out what had happened with Noah. I agreed to put everything behind me, but I told him I didn't want us to take anything out on each other. For Noah's sake, we had to be a team. I kissed Noah good-bye and went back to the Ronald McDonald House, since Noah's dad was going to be staying at the hospital that night. I figured I would go back, shower, eat, and catch up on sleep. The next morning, I woke up and gathered my things and rushed over to the hospital. I wanted to make sure I was there bright and early so I could be there ready when the ombudsman arrived. Once I arrived there, Noah's dad left to go back to the Ronald McDonald House to sleep. I checked in with the nurses to get an update on how Noah was doing. They told me there were no issues and they had given him Tylenol to help him with any discomfort. They also informed me that the wound doctor was going to drop by to check Noah's neck. I kissed Noah and turned on his lullabies for him, since he was still asleep. I grabbed his tiny hand, still in sadness and remorse over what had happened to him. I sang to him and began telling him how at the age of twenty-five, I prayed for him to come. I had always wanted a little boy, and every night I would pray to God, hoping I would find someone I could love and have a son with. I told him that I had dreamed of being with him, and how I was so happy that he was finally here with me. He was all mine to call my own, and despite where we were, I told him I would always love him, fight for him, and he would never be alone. Hours passed and I was becoming hungry, since I was still trying to squeeze in pumping even for any little amount I had. Around noon I informed the nurse I was going to the cafeteria to get lunch and would head right back since I still had to wait for the ombudsman to come. I went to the cafeteria and had my usual: a bacon cheeseburger, curly fries, and a Coke Zero. As I looked around, I noticed the same mom who had been there when we first arrived at the NICU. I wondered what her story was. I saw her there every day, and I never saw anyone with her. I also prayed for her, hoping she would make it out of here. Once I realized it was one o'clock, I headed back to the PICU. Once I walked into the PICU, I entered my son's room and he was lying there purple. I ran to his crib, picked him up, and started hitting his back for stimulation. Once the charge nurse saw what was occurring, she began to bag him. The charge nurse looked at the monitor to see why the alarm was off, since no alarms rang to alert the nurses when he turned purple. Once he came to, he began crying, and I just held him and told him everything was going to be okay. I held him, trying not to scream at the nurses, since I was so infuriated. I began to ask how long he had been purple, and why wasn't anyone checking on him? The DA ran in and stated she heard what had happened and stated she didn't know why the alarms were not working and would go over the monitor screen to see how long he had been purple. After a turning-purple episode, Noah usually passed a bowel movement and went into a deep sleep for hours. I couldn't imagine what an episode like that did to the body, especially with him being a baby and all. Shortly after, the DA came in with a printed paper showing timestamps from when the monitor started silently alarming, and it showed it was only five seconds before I walked in. I asked the DA, if I had not walked in to see him, what would have happened? She said a nurse was always stationed to watch the monitor if they couldn't be in the room. I told her that while there was a nurse in this situation, when I entered the PICU, they were all at a corner desk talking, nowhere near the monitor to observe Noah. The DA told me she would investigate it and left the room. I was livid; I felt so unsafe in this hospital, where I should have felt the most comfort and care. I felt I could no longer leave the room, because no one would watch Noah. I wanted to scream at them and tell them the meanest things possible. It wasn't just the fact that my son was left unmonitored; it was wondering if this was going to be his last breath. Every time he turned purple, I thought, *This is it. Is this going to be a desaturation he doesn't recover from?* I don't wish that on anyone—to see their child turn dark purple and rigid in their arms while trying to stimulate them to come back and trying to suction them, trying to do anything possible to get them to breathe. This was the worst pain imaginable, to see your child in this manner. I had to keep asking myself over and over, *What would Jesus do?* because I felt as if I was going to snap. I prayed for the Lord to humble my heart. No good would come out of fighting; however, all I was seeing was red now, and I wanted to scream and shout at the nurses. Around 3 p.m., the ombudsman entered Noah's room and asked if we were ready for the meeting. I retrieved my notebook with a list of questions and concerns I had regarding the care Noah was receiving and the second-degree burns. As we headed down the hall toward the conference room, my adrenaline began pumping and I could feel my blood begin to boil; however, I kept praying over and over for the Lord to be present with me. I wanted to be able to say the things I needed to say as well as seek the answers I needed, but without screaming at everyone. As we entered the room, everyone was there, including the respiratory therapist supervisor, the DA, the charge nurse, and the acting MD in the PICU. We sat down, and the ombudsman started the meeting by stating who she was and why we were there and what questions we wanted answered regarding what had happened to Noah. The DA started by stating she had spoken with the staff who were present on the night shift the day of the incident, and they reported there was an emergency with another patient on the floor, and per protocol, they had to tend to the emergency at hand until it was sustained. She continued to state that the respiratory therapist as well as the nurse did not have enough time to complete the trach care, and it was reported to the morning shift so they could complete the trach care. I stated I understood the protocol; however, the trach care did not get done until 9 a.m. the next morning, which was four hours after shift change, and there seemed to be no emergency taking place that morning. The respiratory supervisor stated he would speak to his staff regarding better communication skills between the team so matters such as these could be handled more efficiently. The ombudsman stated the next question, which was, Why hadn't it been reported right away when the wound was seen by the staff? The DA responded that according to the chart, staff did report redness in their notes, but that was it. They thought it was due to the recent procedure that was done. I told the DA I understood it was reported, but the staff didn't put how severe it was and how the skin looked as if it were peeling off. There was more than redness. I also went on to state that it wasn't until the respiratory therapist who knew Noah called the nurse and told her to take a picture and send it to the doctor that things were done. The DA stated she was talking to the team in order to develop new procedures to train staff on what to do if an incident like this occurred. She apologized and stated this also could have happened if he was sweating profusely, causing the silver nitrate to drip down his neck. Everyone apologized repeatedly and stated that trainings and staff meetings would be held in order to address this issue. It wasn't the answers I wanted. I wanted someone to be held accountable, I wanted someone to be punished, but I knew the hospital was not going to admit fault, especially since this could be a possible lawsuit. I had no strength to take on something like that, so I knew I would have no justice in this matter. I walked out of that meeting feeling defeated. However, I knew my focus had to be on getting Noah out of the hospital as soon as I could. We had our discharge date for December 15, so I needed to do everything in my power to bring him home. That night I told Noah's dad I was going to clear all my things out of the Ronald McDonald House so I could have everything with me at the hospital. No matter what, I was never going to leave Noah alone again. I didn't trust the hospital anymore.

December 10, 2019

The wound doctor came in just to check the status of Noah's neck before we went home. By this time, it had scabbed and healed completely, not leaving a scar, which we were happy about, including the hospital. The wound doctor said that the neck area should be fine now, and we could go back to cleaning the area with a fifty-fifty solution of sterile water and peroxide. He continued that we could now dab a gauze around the neck and stoma area two times a day. After the doctor left, the nurse informed me we would have a PT session, which would require Noah to be out of the crib and on a play mat. Shortly after the PT arrived, we placed Noah on his Boppy on the play mat and tried tummy time for the first time ever. Noah was so used to being on his back for so long that once we placed him for tummy time, he had no idea what to do and just cried. I felt so bad; he was now two and a half months old, and he had no idea how to be on his tummy. He also had no idea that this world was bigger than just the hospital and his crib. After a bit of tummy time, I placed Noah between my legs and let his head rest on my chest, and I held back tears. This was the first time I sat with my baby between my legs. I made sure I took pictures to mark this day and thanked Jesus for allowing this day to occur. I thanked God for showing me that Noah was a fighter, and there was more to being a NICU mom. There was more bonding yet to come, and this was just the beginning. Later that afternoon, the OT stopped by and apologized for not being available for the past two weeks. I asked her, since Noah's discharge date was around the corner, if we could continue to work on his feeding, since I didn't want him to lose the ability to swallow. She said she would continue to do oral exercises with him as well as show me techniques and massages I could do to help him with the muscles around his mouth. Shortly after, she went to get a bottle with a preemie nipple to try to see if Noah would attempt to swallow his formula. Once she put a drop of formula in his mouth, Noah instantly smiled. As she began to insert the bottle into his mouth, he began choking.

She began to do mouth exercises while the formula was still in his mouth; however, Noah just let it drip out of his mouth. She told me she would have to conduct a blue dye test to ensure he was not aspirating, since he had choked a little. She told me how the blue dye test worked: They would put blue dye in the formula and try to get him to swallow the formula. Then they would immediately suction his trach in order to make sure there was no blue dye in his secretions. If there was blue dye, then it would mean he was aspirating. She told me she would try to conduct the test next week before we left so that the feeding specialist could continue what they were working on after discharge. However, that day never came. The OT became so busy, since she was the only OT in the PICU, that Noah never got to see her or do the blue dye test.

December 14, 2019

We were so close to the discharge date that I became nervous. I was hopeful, but I also did not want to get too carried away in case the discharge date was pushed back for whatever reason. The nurse walked in and told me today I would be doing the twenty-four-hour care for Noah, which was the last step on our training list. Noah's dad would do tomorrow, and then we would be ready to go on the sixteenth. The nurse asked me to bring his stroller and car seat so we could work on how to load him with the vent and all his supplies. Once I retrieved the stroller and carrier, I went straight up to the PICU and began to prep the best way to load Noah into the car seat with his ventilator. The nurse walked me through the best way to load him, and as scared as I was, I just went for it. I put him in, making sure the ventilator circuit was safely wrapped around the stroller handle, with it connected to Noah. Then I placed his emergency bag with him. When we first placed him in the car seat, he seemed uncomfortable, since it was a new position, but also curious. As soon as he was strapped in, we took him for a walk around the PICU ward. All the nurses were smiling and saying he was finally getting to go home and how brave and strong he was. He seemed to be comfortable and was just looking around as if asking, What is going on? We went twice around the PICU, then went back to his room. Again the nurses walked me through how to unload Noah while he was connected to the ventilator. I placed him back in his bed and he began to cry. I rubbed his head and told him in two days he would be home in his own bed, so not to worry. As nighttime came, I got dressed in my pajamas and got ready to continue the twenty-four-hour care. It had already started at 6 a.m., but since I had done everything throughout the day, they wanted to make sure I got up throughout the night, since he ate every three hours. It was so easy for me to do; I just did exactly what I had done during the day. That night I went to bed at 12 a.m., praying to God that this would be over and we would be home and would be a happy family. I dozed off to bed and woke up around 2:45 to get Noah's 3 a.m. feeding ready. As I set it up, I finally felt like a full-time mom, getting up to feed him, in and out of sleep, changing diapers. No matter the case, I felt so happy. This was all I had ever wanted—Noah and I living like a normal mom-and-baby situation. As soon as I was done, I couldn't go back to sleep, so I waited in a chair next to his crib while I watched him sleep until his feeding was done, since it ran over an hour. At 4 a.m., I decided to go to bed. I woke up at 5:45 to change his diaper, check his temperature, and set up his feeding for 6 a.m. Around 6:30 a.m., the shift nurse walked in and told me I had completed the twenty-four-hour care and everything went well. Around 7 a.m., Noah's dad walked in with his overnight bag and told the nurse he would now be starting his twenty-four-hour care. Once he settled in, I kissed Noah good-bye and told his dad I was going back to our apartment to do last-minute things for Noah, since he had already gone back the day before to clean. As I left the hospital and did the hour-and-a-half commute home, everything felt weird. It felt like an eternity since I had driven on the 14 freeway, and once I entered my town and parked at the apartment, it felt weird being there. As I unlocked the door, I entered the apartment and noticed Noah's dad had decorated the house for the holidays. I was so happy. I had thought we weren't going to make it home in time for Christmas, so I didn't even think about decorating and figured we would try to do it once Noah was home. The whole apartment had Christmas lights and a little tree with ornaments and red and green everywhere. As I walked down the hallway, I stopped at Noah's door, knowing I had to go in to make sure everything was good for his arrival. As I took a deep breath, I opened the door and entered the room. It was just exactly how I had left it, except now with a desk in the corner. I made sure his drawers were stocked with diapers and Desitin. I looked through the closet and noticed most of the stuff in there would not fit him, since they were newborn to three months. So I put everything that didn't fit him into a bag and cried. A lot of the things I had bought hoping they would be his first outfit, Halloween attire, and different outfits from the Disney store. I tried to cheer up, but a wave of emotion came over me, and I hugged his clothes and cried. I told myself to get up, snap out of it, and remember the positive—we were almost out of there. I sat in the rocking chair and took a deep breath and thought that in two days I would have Noah in my arms, rocking him to sleep. I went to the bedroom, turned on the TV, and went to sleep. Once I woke up, it was almost 9 p.m. I messaged Noah's dad and thanked him for decorating, and I told him I would be there at 6 a.m. to get ready for the discharge. We never talked about being together, but I took it as a peace offering. Maybe this would be the turning stone to be on good terms.

December 16, Date of Discharge

I woke up at 3:30 a.m., took a shower, and got ready. I went to Starbucks to get a coffee, and I was smiling. I couldn't believe today was the day my life was going to change—my Noah was coming home. I drove down to LA, listening to worship music and praying to God, thanking Him so much for this day. As I arrived at the hospital, Noah's dad was there with the nurses, and they were discussing possible discharge times. The nurse looked at me and informed me that discharge was usually around noon. She told me she would get the process started and call the paramedics, since he would be transported home via ambulance. They would also need to inform the home respiratory therapist to meet us at the hospital to go over supplies and follow us home, just in case. Noah's dad told me he would go back to the apartment to make sure the in-home nurse was there when we arrived and get last-minute preparations done. I agreed, and the nurse left to start the discharge process. I put on his going-home outfit and told him we were going to go home. I kept pacing back and forth, anxious about everything. I messaged my family and told them the great news. Everyone was so excited and thanked God for our miracle and said congrats. Shortly after, the acting doctor told me that overnight, while doing the trach care with Dad, they noticed Noah had growing granulomas and contacted the ENT doctor just to make sure there would be no issues or blockage of the trach site. They told me the doctor should be in around 12 p.m., and from there we could go home. I felt as if the time was dragging. At 11 a.m., the in-home respiratory therapist dropped by and told me he would be leaving a travel vent with me so Noah could be connected to it once we left the hospital. He told me he would follow us in the ambulance to make sure everything was okay and give us the rest of the equipment Noah needed, such as a pulse oximeter and suction machine. At the time, I had no idea what those were, but I just nodded my head and agreed. Around 12 p.m., I sat there waiting, hoping for the doctor to come in to get the show on the road, but nothing. Every time the PICU doors opened, I hoped it was the doctor; however, it was now 2 p.m., when the nurse walked in and told me that unfortunately, the ENT had been in surgery all day and had not had time to drop by. The case manager walked in and handed me paperwork detailing all Noah's equipment and the supplies he would be receiving and the paperwork I needed for the electric and fire department. I asked the case manager, being how late it was, would we still get discharged, and she said unfortunately, they had spoken with the team and Noah would not be getting discharged until tomorrow morning when the ENT could make it. My heart broke. I wanted to cry; I had nothing with me but a bag. I had been telling Noah all morning we would be gone, but I was stuck here. I nodded my head, and she hugged me and told me it was okay and tomorrow was the day. I went back to by Noah's crib and just hung my head and cried. I called Noah's dad and told him everything, and that tomorrow we would be discharged. I put on Noah's worship lullabies and sang along with them. I didn't want the negative feelings to consume me so I, prayed: *Lord, for whatever reason, You didn't allow it to happen today. Let me trust You in this process and know You are here for me and my son. Please let this day end quickly, and get us home. In Jesus' name, amen.* After the prayer, I swore to myself I would be happy and positive and focus on just spending time with Noah. Around 8 p.m., I left the hospital to get some fresh air. I walked down the street to eat quickly and headed back to be with Noah. That night I put my head on the mattress of his crib, holding his hand, and I fell asleep. The next morning, I was awoken by the morning shift change. I was still in the same clothes I had worn yesterday and asked the nurse for a disposable toothbrush so I could freshen up for the day. Luckily, I had packed two outfits in Noah's diaper bag and began to change him into fresh clothes. That morning I didn't tell him anything regarding discharge. I didn't want to get my hopes up again. I picked him up out of the crib and rocked him in my arms and sang to him. Around 8 a.m., the doctor and nurses did rounds and told me the ENT was already on her way, and they had already ordered the ambulance transport. I smiled and said thank you. My heart began to flutter, and I felt at peace. No anxiety, no being scared—this was finally happening. Thank the Lord! Shortly after, the ENT walked in and apologized over and over for not being able to come yesterday. She took a look at his granulomas and told me they were big but could be monitored at home, and she would prescribe steroid drops to put on the granulomas so they could decrease in size. She congratulated me on going home and told me all the specialists would follow us every three months, and all the appointments had already been set up. I thanked her so much for everything, and she told Noah good-bye. Once she left, the nurse and case manager walked in and told me they had informed the respiratory therapist to come to the hospital to be ready to follow us home. The nurse began detaching all equipment from Noah—his leads, his pulse ox, and his IV. My son was finally cord free. I felt so happy to see him there with no wires on him. Once all the wires were removed, they transitioned him to the travel ventilator that required no connection to an outlet and the pulse oximeter so we could watch his vitals. The case manager told me the EMTs were on their way and should be here in ten minutes, so she would get the discharge paperwork so Noah would be good to go. As soon as she left, in walked the travel respiratory therapist who would be following us home in the ambulance. He showed me how to put the pulse ox sensor around Noah's foot and gave me extra to hold on to, just in case. I called Noah's dad to inform him we were on our way, and I texted the group chat and sent a picture to my family of Noah being placed in his car seat and tied to the gurney. I was half crying from happiness. This was it—this was our time to leave; it was finally here. I was leaving to go home with my son, and it was all thanks to Jesus Christ, my Savior. We started walking out of the PICU. I had three bags in my hand, and I waved good-bye to everyone. The nurses and doctors stood at the door, all saying good-bye and good luck.

We walked out the back of the hospital, and Noah and I sat behind in the ambulance. I gave them my home address and we were off. I held Noah's hand during the whole ride, praying and hoping we arrived home safely. As soon as we hit the 14 freeway, I knew this was it. This chapter of my life was closing, and I could begin my life again. When we arrived at the apartment complex with Noah in hand, I entered the door and at last we were home. The gloom was over; the light at the end of the tunnel was finally here. I was going to have my little family back, going to live a normal life, and, most importantly, get back what was stolen from me—my dream. However, if I knew then what I know now, I would say this was only the beginning. I would tell myself then that it's okay, you are going to make it, have faith and hope, and your time will come. Always rely on God, and most importantly, view yourself as He views you, which is a strong woman given the task to raise your warrior. You're not alone, you can do this. "Never will I leave you; never will I forsake you" (Heb. 13:5).

CPSIA information can be obtained
at www.ICGtesting.com
Printed in the USA
BVHW021105020323
659503BV00016B/99

9 781662 872303